DATING DIFFERENTLY

DATING DIFFERENTLY

A GUIDE TO REFORMED DATING

JOSHUA ENGELSMA

REFORMED
FREE PUBLISHING
ASSOCIATION
Jenison, Michigan

Reformed Free Publishing Association
1894 Georgetown Center Drive
Jenison, Michigan 49428
616-457-5970
rfpa.org
mail@rfpa.org

Cover design by Amy Zevenbergen
Interior design by Katherine Lloyd / theDESKonline.com

ISBN: 978-1-944555-59-7 (hardcover)
ISBN: 978-1-944555-60-3 (ebook)
LCCN: 2019944851

To Courtney,
beloved wife and selfless mother,
and the one with whom
all these lessons were learned.

CONTENTS

PREFACE

A note about the title of this book: *Dating Differently*. The title is not intended to convey that I've discovered some new method that will revolutionize dating forever. I haven't. It simply expresses the thread that ties the whole book together: as Christians, we aren't governed by the attitudes and thinking of the world in any area of life, this one included. That is, we date, but we do so differently, as those guided by God's word.

I believe this book has value, if for nothing else than to get you thinking about this important subject. Perhaps you'll disagree with some of the practical suggestions I make. No problem. I realize that in some ways what I write might be considered "idealistic." But I do hope this main thought sticks with you: as Christians, we date differently than the world around us. And I hope that what I've written here gets you to stop and think carefully about what that means in your life.

This book is short. Intentionally so. No doubt there is much more that could be said about dating from a Christian perspective. The reason for it being so brief is not that I'm selling you short and thinking that today's youth can't handle something longer. I'm sure you can. But I think there is value in a short book that gets right to the point, that hits some of the highlights of dating, and that gets you thinking.

There are plenty of other books on dating on the market, some worthwhile, others not. In part what makes this book unique is that it is written from the viewpoint of the biblical, historically Reformed view of marriage as the union of one man and one woman for life, with divorce permitted only in cases of fornication and all remarriage forbidden while one's spouse is living. This precious truth, still maintained in the Protestant Reformed Churches in which I serve, is applied in the pages that follow to the practical subject of dating.

My prayer is that God might use what I've written here in a small way to encourage godly dating relationships and strong marriages.

One final note: all of the names and some of the details in the stories I reference have been changed to protect the identity and privacy of those about whom I'm speaking. Consider these examples to be just that, examples, as you might make use of their themes and underlying principles to inform your own dating life.

CHAPTER 1

IS THERE HELP?

Every young person could use help in the area of dating. Some might need it more than others, but all need it. No, I'm not talking about needing help getting a date (although maybe some of you feel that way). What I have in mind instead is that everyone needs help thinking properly about dating.

I hope you've taken this book in hand because you are conscious of your need for help and you desire that help. I hope you are already asking the right questions and looking in the right places for the answers.

But I'm guessing that some of you really don't feel like you need help. Maybe you aren't thinking seriously about dating. Maybe you have a touch of overconfidence and find yourself saying, "What's the big deal? Do I really need a book to tell me how to date? I think I can figure this out on my own." I hope that's not true, but I'm not so out of touch as to think that's impossible.

In this opening chapter, I hope to establish the need for a proper perspective on dating, and then to lay out in broad terms what assistance we have. For those who already know their need, I trust these are things you have been thinking about. And for those who don't think they need help, I hope this introduction whets your appetite for what follows.

OUR GUIDE: NEEDED

The way I see it, there are three reasons why the Christian young person might need help with the subject of dating.

1. This guidance is necessary because of the influence of the ungodly world.

The world in the twenty-first century has adopted certain practices for dating. A young man and young woman start to date because they sense an attraction to one another. There is no consideration of age or where the other person is at spiritually. There is no consideration of where this relationship is headed. It is based almost exclusively on hormones and feelings.

If this first relationship doesn't end up working out, the young person quickly moves on to someone else. In the course of their time in high school and college, young people might date dozens of different people, leaving a string of breakups in their wake.

4

In worldly dating, the main interest is sex. It is expected that at some point in high school a young person will lose his or her virginity. It is not a question of if but a question of when, and the world does not see this as a problem. The main problem they see is if a young woman has an accidental and unwanted pregnancy. For that reason their concerns in "sex education" are merely to warn against unprotected sex, to hand out condoms, and to pressure young women to start taking birth control.

After a couple has been exclusive for a while, they are encouraged to live together. Maybe they view this as a trial run, in order to be sure that they really want to get married. Maybe they feel like they aren't ready for marriage yet because they are in college or because they aren't financially secure. Maybe they view marriage as an outdated institution that has outgrown its use. So they share an apartment or even buy a house and move in together.

The world's view of dating is essentially lawlessness. In this area also they show themselves to be a "crooked and perverse nation" (Phil. 2:15). They are not governed by the objective standard of God's word. They aren't even governed by old-fashioned traditional values or by the wishes of their parents. They are ruled by their wants, desires, and emotions. They are their own god in the sphere of dating.

This attitude toward dating is spread by heavy propaganda. The stories are trending on social media and can be found splashed across the covers of gossip rags in the checkout aisle. Neighbors and coworkers promote it through their actions and conversation. Movies, music, and literature encourage it.

There is no denying that the world's attitude toward dating has an influence upon Christian young people. The world creeps closer and closer to the church, especially through technology, particularly social media, and this creates pressure upon the youth of the church to conform to the thinking of the world. Conformity to the world might come consciously, but also unconsciously. Without even knowing it, we can begin to think and talk and act like our peers in the world.

The reality of this pressure and influence requires that we have our thinking rebooted and reset. Romans 12:2 says, "Be not conformed to this world: but be ye transformed by the renewing of your mind." So that we are not conformed to the world's ideas for dating, we need our minds renewed. In this, we need help. As you progress through this book, you will find that turning to scripture is the way God would have us renew our minds.

2. This guidance is necessary because of the difficulty of dating.

Entirely apart from the influence of the world upon you as young people, there is need for instruction on this subject because of the difficulty of dating. To radically understate the case, dating is not easy.

A young person might have questions about "the right time" to start dating. Sixteen? Eighteen? Should I date in high school? Should I start dating when I have four more years of college to go?

Or you might have questions about whom to date. What should I be looking for in a boyfriend or girlfriend? What if I'm dating this person but I'm not sure they're "the one"? What should I do if I'm asked out by someone I don't really have an attraction to?

Some other difficult questions might arise while considering dating. Is "dating" even appropriate? Should I consider courtship? What even is courtship? Where are we going to go? What are we going to do? What are we going to talk about all night? And then, what about sex? Where are the boundaries? How far is too far? How do things change if we've been dating for several years or are engaged?

Other questions matter more once you've been dating for a while. When is the right time to get married? What if I'm in college? What if I have a lot of debt? What if I'm ready but he's not? What will marriage be like?

This is just a small sample of the questions you might face regarding dating. And that doesn't even begin to address all the questions and concerns that parents might have in the business of dating.

The difficulty of dating is evident from the great harm that can be done through it. One Reformed pastor was spot-on when he wrote, "More harm comes to many of us through dating than in any other way."[1] Think about how many people walk away from dating with deep regrets, guilty consciences, or the emotional pain of a bad breakup.

The fact that dating is difficult makes it a subject of great interest for young people (and their parents). It is something that young people regularly ask to discuss in Bible study societies, something they want to read about in blogs and articles, and something they talk about frequently with each other. It is something that parents also discuss between themselves and with others, and it is one of the great fears that they have as their children get older.

The difficulty of dating itself, especially with the pressure of the world added to it, means that we need help thinking properly about dating.

3. This guidance is necessary because of how monumental marriage is.

The decision to get married is one of the most significant decisions that a child of God could ever make. It is far more important than deciding what college to attend, or what career to pursue, or what city to live in. The only decision that is possibly more important is the decision about what church to attend. But other than that, the decision about whom to marry is the most momentous decision you can make.

---

1   Richard D. & Sharon L. Phillips, *Holding Hands, Holding Hearts: Recovering a Biblical View of Christian Dating* (Phillipsburg, NJ: P&R Publishing, 2006), 14.

There are many reasons why this is true. One reason is that marriage is for life. You might struggle to decide where to live or what career to pursue, but those things can always change. Not so with marriage. This is a choice that, once done, cannot be undone.

Another reason why marriage is so momentous is that the person you marry will shape and mold the person that you become. A young woman who marries a spiritually weak young man might find herself becoming spiritually weak as well. A young man who marries an independent, domineering wife might find that he is no longer the head of his house. In contrast, a young person married to a spiritually-minded spouse might find himself or herself growing in faith and godliness. Our spouse is one of the most powerful tools God uses in our sanctification.

The person whom you marry will also play an important role in shaping and molding your future children, if the Lord gives them. The young man you marry will one day be the father of your children and be called upon to lead them spiritually. The young woman you marry will one day be the mother of your children and be called upon to nurture and care for them throughout the day.

Marriage is not a joke. It is not some careless decision to be made on a whim or at the spur of the moment. Marriage is serious business!

Because marriage is so important, by implication dating is also serious business. The process of seeking a spouse and determining the Lord's will regarding marriage is equally as important. For that reason it's important that we think carefully about dating.

OUR GUIDE: IDENTIFIED

It should come as no surprise to the Christian young person that the place where we turn for help in our dating is the word of God. The inspired scriptures must be our guide as we look for a spouse.

But perhaps this does come as a surprise to you. Maybe you're wondering, "How can the Bible help? It never says anything about dating. This is just a matter of Christian liberty, right? Which means that we just have to figure things out on our own."

Yes, it's certainly true that the Bible never mentions the word "dating" or describes anything remotely close to modern dating. But that doesn't mean that the word of God should sit on a shelf collecting dust while we search for answers to our dating questions. Without directly addressing the subject, the word has much to say that applies to dating.

In Reformed theology we refer to this as the truth of the sufficiency of scripture. This means that the Bible contains everything that we need to know for what we believe (faith) and how we conduct ourselves (life). The Bible is sufficient to address every need of the child of God. Second Timothy 3:16–17 says, "All scripture is given by inspiration of God, and is profitable...for instruction in righteousness: that the man of God may be perfect, throughly furnished unto all good works."

The Bible lays out fundamental principles in many areas of life, even though it does not address them specifically. It does not specifically address watching TV, but it certainly has something to say about the amount of time we spend in front of it and the things we watch. It does not specifically address smoking, but it certainly has something to say about addictions and idolatry and harming our bodies. Many more examples could be given, but the main point is this: the word is relevant for all of life, which includes dating.

The Bible does address the all-important question of whom we are to marry. It gives guiding principles for the involvement of parents in the dating of their young people. It provides clear instructions and warnings about sex in dating. It holds before the young person the ultimate goal of dating: marriage. Let's not sell God's word short.

In the following chapters, I hope to spell out the main principles of God's word that ought to guide us in our dating. I will include practical implications and advice along the way, but the main thing to consider is how the scripture shines its light upon the pathway to marriage.

OUR GUIDE: TIMELESS

If we have these principles of scripture to guide the way, the things we say here ought to hold true for every generation.

If the word is timeless, its basic principles concerning dating ought to be timeless as well.

There are always going to be specific things that change in dating, as has been the case throughout history. We see evidence of this in the different practices spoken of in the Bible. For example, the Bible mentions arranged marriages. Think of Abraham sending his servant to find a wife for Isaac (Gen. 24). There was no such thing then as our modern concept of dating. Often, the father of a young man would approach the father of a young woman, the two would haggle over an appropriate dowry, and then they would arrange the marriage of their children. The son and daughter were often informed of the arrangement after the fact.

However, arranged marriages were not the rule. It was possible for a young man and young woman to develop an interest in one another and then look to their parents for approval. Think about how Jacob approached Laban for Rachel's hand in marriage.

The Bible also mentions being "espoused," such as with Joseph and Mary (Matt. 1:18). This was much more than an engagement. The two were considered married and even spoke vows to one another to that effect. But they then waited a year before consummating their marriage sexually. They prepared a home for themselves, and after a year had passed they consummated their marriage and were considered husband and wife.

The differences in dating practices over time are something we can especially see from the last century in America.[2] A very different kind of "dating" was practiced during the 1800s and the early 1900s. A young man might have a special interest in a young woman, but he had to make that interest known to both sets of parents. Then he needed an invitation to "call" on her at her home. Either the couple would attend a church or community function together, or they would spend time at her home under the watchful eye of her parents.

Then things changed during the 1920s and 30s. More young people had access to automobiles, and therefore dating gradually shifted from the private sphere of the home to the public sphere.

Another dramatic shift took place during the middle of the twentieth century, especially after the end of World War II. At this time there was a dramatic increase in the availability of transportation, entertainment, and disposable income. These things made it even easier for young couples to spend time outside of the parental home. Dating came to mean spending time alone with just each other and without the oversight of dad and mom.

The 1960s saw the development of the sexual revolution, which had a powerful influence on dating. Dating became equated with sex, which could happen without the fear of an

---

2   For more on the history of dating, see Alex and Marni Chediak, *With One Voice: Singleness, Dating, and Marriage to the Glory of God* (Fearn, Scotland: Christian Focus, 2006), 13–25. Chediak is dependent on Beth Bailey, *From Front Porch to Back Seat: Courtship in Twentieth-Century America* (Baltimore, MD: Johns Hopkins University Press, 1989).

unwanted pregnancy due to the increased availability of birth control and abortion. In addition, dating was disconnected from marriage and characterized by rebellion against the authority and oversight of parents.

Today it's not uncommon for a young man and young woman to start dating without their parents' knowledge. Only after they've dated for a while are their parents informed. They might spend several years dating, usually by going off on their own without parental oversight. Eventually there is an engagement, followed several months later by the public event of the wedding.

As this brief summary shows, there have been many different "dating" practices throughout history. Undoubtedly, things will continue to change in coming years. But amidst all these changes, what ought to guide us is not what our emotions or modern culture dictates. We must have the word as our timeless guide. It will not address every how-to of dating. Some things are left to sanctified common sense. But the main principles of God's word ought to hold true. In the next chapter, let's look at one of those principles.

DISCUSSION QUESTIONS

1. What are some of the things that make dating difficult?

2. Why is getting married one of the most important decisions in your life?

3. What is one thing in this chapter that taught you how to date differently from the world?

4. How is the Bible a guide to your dating? Before you begin the next chapter, find two or three Bible passages that speak to modern dating. Why did you choose these passages? What do you learn from them?

CHAPTER 2

WHERE'S THIS HEADED?

Jack and Kate have dated for several years. They started when they were both juniors in high school. Jack is now in his second year at a local college, while Kate is finishing up her program to become a dental hygienist. They get along well with each other, and each is welcomed by the other's family.

One Saturday afternoon, Jack is playing a round of golf with a couple of his high school friends. While they wait for a group in front of them to get off the green, one of Jack's friends says, "So, you and Kate have been dating for a while now. Where are you guys headed? Ever think about when you're going to get married?"

Jack laughs nervously. He doesn't admit it, but he really hasn't given much thought to the future. "We're too young for marriage, and I've got a lot of school left," he says, then changes the subject.

That same afternoon, Kate is spending time with her older sister, with whom she is very close. In the course of conversation, Kate's sister says, "So, you and Jack have been dating for a while now. Where are you guys headed? Ever think about when you're going to get married?"

Kate laughs nervously. "We haven't really talked about it," she confides. "We're still pretty young, and Jack has a lot of school left, so it probably won't be for a while."

That night Jack picks up Kate for a date. In time, he recognizes that Kate seems nervous and distant.

"Is something wrong?" Jack asks.

"Well…I was talking to my sister today, and she made me think about where we're going. Where are we heading?"

"I thought we'd try that new restaurant on the south side. I heard it was pretty good."

Kate sighs, struggling to mask her frustration. "I don't mean, where are we going out to eat? I mean, where is this relationship headed?"

"I don't know," Jack admits with a touch of embarrassment. "What do you think?"

"I don't know either."

THE END FROM THE BEGINNING

I wonder how close to reality Jack and Kate's example hits for many Christians who are dating. Ambiguity is certainly a reality for most unbelievers in their dating. Dating for them is without purpose or direction, merely a time for pleasure and self-satisfaction.

What ought to make our dating different from the world is that we date with a purpose, and that's what I want to discuss in this chapter: the goal of Christian dating. Where ought these relationships to be heading? What ought we to be aiming toward?

The simple answer to that question is marriage. The end that we have in mind in all Christian dating must be the holy institution of marriage.

This might seem a bit backward. Why in a book on dating would we begin by talking about marriage? You might wonder, "If you're going to talk about marriage at all, shouldn't that come at the very end of the book? Shouldn't the last thing be treated…well, last? Why the end from the beginning?"

But there's good reason to treat the end from the beginning. In fact, I'm convinced that marriage is so essential that it's the only appropriate way to begin the dating discussion. I have two main reasons for this conviction.

First, we have to begin with the ending because dating must be purposeful. I'll have more to say on this in the next chapter, so I won't elaborate on it here. But for dating to be done right, that is, for dating to be glorifying to God, it must be consciously guided and directed toward the goal of marriage. Jack and Kate may have had a holy and admirable relationship up to this point, but there was a serious flaw.

They both should have known from the beginning how to answer the question, "Where is this headed?"

Second, we have to begin with marriage not only because it is the goal toward which the relationship is heading, but also because it governs every aspect of dating. The truth of marriage rules the things that we do in our preparation for marriage. The things that I say in the rest of this chapter will serve as the foundation and measure for almost everything else I say in the book.

Take just one example. God says that when a Christian marries, he may marry only another Christian. He must marry "only in the Lord" (1 Cor. 7:39). This truth concerning marriage has a whole host of implications for our dating. If we may marry only another Christian, then we will date only another Christian. If we may marry only in the Lord, then we are limited in where we will look for a date: not at the local bar or on the worldly dating site, but in the church, the Christian school, and our Christian communities. This is just one example of how the truth of marriage governs dating.

For these two reasons, it's essential that we begin at the end.

IN THE BEGINNING...

The best place to start in understanding marriage is God's institution of marriage in Genesis 2. If you want a proper understanding of any truth, you have to know its origin. What was its original purpose? How was it designed? This passage records the original institution of marriage by God and reveals to us the will of God for us in marriage from the beginning.

The events recorded in Genesis 2 took place on the sixth day of creation. On the third day God had planted the garden of Eden with its two important trees, and on the sixth day God made the land animals and Adam and placed them in the garden.

But there was one thing missing yet in paradise: a woman. The constant refrain throughout Genesis 1 is "it was very good," but in Genesis 2:18 God says to himself, "It is not good." He says, "It is not good that the man should be alone." Literally, he says, "It is not good that the man be in his separation." Adam was not just alone, but he was separated from someone else who belonged with him. He didn't fully understand who that other was, but he was lacking another human being who was his complement.

God made Adam know this need by bringing to him all the animals. At first we might wonder why reference to the animals is inserted here in the story, but the purpose of God in doing so was to make Adam sense his need for a woman. God brought the animals to Adam in the garden so that Adam could give them their names. As Adam gave them their names, he recognized that they came to him in pairs. There was a male and female lion, a male and female horse, a male and female eagle. In this way God made Adam conscious of his lack. He began to sense that he was incomplete and missing a partner. Verse 20 says, "But for Adam there was not found an help meet for him."

It was important that Adam knew and felt his incompleteness. This knowledge would make a difference in the way that Adam received his wife from God and the way in which he treated her. If God had made Adam and his wife at the exact same moment, Adam would not have appreciated her as he ought. He might view her as unnecessary and dispensable. But having been made conscious of his need and feeling deeply his loneliness, Adam would now appreciate his wife and value her highly as his complement.

After making Adam know his need, God then supplied his need by creating the woman. Verse 21 says, "The LORD God caused a deep sleep to fall upon Adam, and he slept." God did not do this in order to keep Adam from feeling pain when he took one of his ribs. This wasn't an anesthetic before God performed surgery. This sleep indicated that God was going to perform one last creative work and that it would be a work in which man was not engaged. On all the other days of creation, no one was there to witness, much less participate in, the work of God. The same must be true here; this work was God's work alone in which man had no part.

After he put Adam to sleep, God took one of his ribs. Verse 22 says, "The rib, which the LORD God had taken from man, made he a woman." It was necessary that the woman be made out of the man because of the headship of Adam. If the woman was made separately out of the dust of the ground as the man was, there would be two separate heads of the human race. But God had set Adam as the one head of the human race, and from him would come the woman and the whole rest of mankind. So God took one of the ribs of Adam, and from that rib he built the woman.

After creating the woman, God then brought her to Adam in the first marriage ceremony. This was not only the first marriage, but it was also the institution of marriage as an enduring ordinance among men.

BASICS FROM THE BEGINNING

From this institution of marriage, we learn six important truths about marriage that also will have application to dating. I'll mention the applications only briefly, as we'll return to many of them in later chapters.

1. Marriage is a divine institution.

The fundamental truth about marriage that comes out in Genesis 2 is that marriage is divinely designed. God is the one who created marriage and therefore rules in marriage.

The world thinks that marriage is a man-made institution. This is the natural conclusion of the teaching of evolutionism. If there was no first man and woman created by God, then the first marriage also becomes a myth. To unbelieving eyes, marriage becomes merely an institution created by some of the first evolved humans as a way of giving order to society and protecting children. If marriage is a man-made institution, then man rules in marriage and may do whatever he pleases. This is the explanation for the rampant godlessness regarding marriage today. Every man and woman is doing what is right in his or her own eyes. In this, they find justification for fornication, for unbiblical divorce and remarriage, for homosexual unions, for people saying that marriage has passed its time of usefulness, and even for rejecting it altogether.

But marriage was instituted and designed by God. That means that God is the one who rules in marriage. God is the one who determines how we are to live in marriage, not worldly psychology or what we see on TV or social media. This means that for a husband and wife, how they live in marriage is not up to them and what feels good or what is easiest. But how they live in marriage must be in submission to the God who created it.

What does this mean for dating? If marriage is ruled by God, dating is ruled by him as well. We aren't governed by the standards of the world in our dating, but by the standard of the word.

2. Marriage is a picture of the relationship between Christ and the church.

In Ephesians 5:31, the inspired apostle quotes from Genesis 2, and in the very next verse he writes, "This [marriage] is a great mystery: but I speak concerning Christ and the church" (v. 32).

When we think about a mystery, we think about something that we cannot figure out, some incomprehensible puzzle or riddle. It is true that there is something mysterious about marriage. Words cannot adequately describe this relationship. One of the things "too wonderful for me" is "the way of a man with a maid" (Prov. 30:18–19).

But that is not what the word *mystery* means here. The mystery refers to God's eternal plan of salvation, which was hidden before but has now been revealed in Christ by the gospel. The great mystery is not some deep, unsolved problem, but it is the salvation of God, which is marvelous and wonderful. The idea is that earthly marriage is designed by God to picture the marriage of Christ and his bride.

Consider briefly the wonder of this union:

◆ The union between Christ and his church is *intimate*. This amazing intimacy is mentioned in Ephesians 5:30: "For we are members of his body, of his flesh, and of his bones." So close is our union to Christ that we are his body and he is our head. He is in us, and we are in him.

◆ The union between Christ and his church is *complementary*. Being united to Christ does not mean that we become Christ. He remains the head and we remain the body (Eph. 5:23). This means that there are different roles in our relationship. He is the head and husband, and therefore he rules over us in love (v. 25). We are the bride, and therefore we submit to him and serve him in love (v. 24).

◆ The union between Christ and his church is *exclusive*. There is no room for any other in this relationship (Song of Sol. 2:16). As our husband, he is faithful to us always. He demands of us as his wife that we be faithful to him always.

◆ The union between Christ and his church is *permanent*. In spite of our sins and unfaithfulness, Christ remains committed to us. He has promised that he will never leave us or forsake us (Heb. 13:5).

Marriage is intended by God to be a reflection of this heavenly union. This means that the purpose of marriage is to teach us about this union. Our earthly marriages are momentary. What I mean is that all marriages will eventually end in death. There is no marriage in heaven. Matthew 22:30 says, "For in the resurrection they neither marry, nor are given in marriage, but are as the angels of God in heaven." But when marriage ends, the real heavenly marriage will continue. This means that marriage has a purpose only for this life. There will come a day when the reality is complete and the picture will not be necessary. The purpose of marriage now is to teach us about the union we have with Christ. It is the clearest and best earthly picture of that spiritual and invisible reality.

This is important for those who are married or want to be married to remember. The point of your marriage is not your love or your happiness. The point of your marriage is to teach you both about what you have in Christ. Your marriage is a witness to yourselves, to your children, and to others of the love that Christ has for his church.

Our marriages are to be patterned after this union. We can profit from books and conferences on marriage, but when it comes down to it there is really only this one piece of advice that is necessary: live in marriage like Christ and the church. Pattern every part of your marriage after that marriage. When you do this, there will be peace and happiness in your marriage. But above all your marriage will glorify God, which is the ultimate purpose of marriage.

How does all this apply to dating? It means that we date only in the Lord: that is, fellow Christians. It means that when we consider whom to date, our chief concern is how they will affect our relationship to Christ. It means that we date for the glory of God.

3. Marriage is for life.

Jesus makes this point in Matthew 19:6. In the context Jesus is answering the tempting question of the Pharisees concerning divorce and remarriage. Jesus answers by going back to the institution of marriage in Genesis 2, and he says, "Wherefore they are no more twain, but one flesh. *What therefore God hath joined together, let not man put asunder*" (emphasis added). Jesus says that although Moses suffered them to divorce—meaning that he did not approve of it but only gave restrictions when he knew it was going on—God from the beginning said otherwise. God from the beginning joined them together as one flesh. This means that man may not put asunder what God has joined together.

Marriage is permanent. God is the one who joins husband and wife together. The glue of marriage is God's glue. He is the only one able to take two and make them one.

Because God joins them together as one, we may not try to break them apart by divorce. God hates divorce! God gives only one ground for divorce, and that is adultery. But even adultery does not break the marriage bond. It may so severely damage the bond that husband and wife cannot live together. But in the eyes of God they are still married.

This means that as long as both spouses are living, they may not remarry. To get an unbiblical divorce is sin, and to remarry is sin. The only one who can break apart the marriage bond is God, and the only way in which he does so is by death. What God has joined together, let not man put asunder!

This needs repeating in our day because of the ever-rising rate of divorce, not just in the world but within the church. Marriages are under attack like never before, and more and more we see the sad breakup of marriages and families.

What does this say about dating? It means dating is not a game but is serious business. The person whom we date and marry is the person we are going to be joined to "for better or worse, till death do us part."

4. Marriage is the union of one man and one woman, each with different roles.

It is almost shameful that I have to state this, but even this most basic and fundamental truth about marriage is denied in today's world. There is rampant divorce and remarriage, so that over the course of one's life he or she might have had many different spouses. In addition, we see the corruption of this truth by the acceptance of homosexual marriages. The devil is unleashing in this country a constant barrage of lies, trying to convince the young person that marriage can be between a man and a man or between a woman and a woman, and the world is swallowing the lies fast enough to choke on them. Everywhere you turn—on social media, on the Internet, on the TV shows and commercials, even in the newspaper—this is portrayed as something normal.

But to understand what marriage is, we must go back to the beginning. The biblical institution of marriage makes plain that marriage is not between one man and many different women or one woman and many different men. The biblical institution of marriage makes plain that marriage is not between one man and another man or between one woman and another woman. Genesis 2 shows us that marriage is the union of one man and one woman.

Genesis 2 also shows us that the man and woman have

different roles to fill in marriage. Unity in marriage is not the same as absolute uniformity. In creating the woman, God did not make a mere replica of the man. He made another human being, but one who is different from the man in important ways. He made the differences of the woman to correspond to and complement the man. First Corinthians 11:8–9 says that the woman was made *out of* the man and *for* the man. First Peter 3:7 says that the wife is a "weaker vessel," which implies that the husband is the stronger vessel and therefore different from her.

God made them with obvious physical differences that complement each other. He made them with mental and emotional differences. Men and women have different dispositions that complement each other. In addition, God designed them in such a way to fill different roles and to carry out different kinds of work.

Many today deny these differences because of the influence of the women's liberation movement. Members of this movement wrongly react to both real and perceived oppression of women by saying that men and women are basically the same without any differences, in so doing emasculating men and defeminizing women.

But such a reaction is wrong. Yes, from the point of view of salvation, men and women are the same. But God made them to be earthly complements of each other. Rather than something unfair and oppressive, this truth is meant to be a rich blessing in marriage.

How does this truth apply to dating? It means there will be different roles in dating, with the man taking the lead. It also means that when we look for a spouse, we are looking for one who will complement us by carrying out the different callings of husband and wife.

5. Marriage is a one-flesh union.

According to Genesis 2:24, marriage is two becoming "one flesh." The mystery of marriage is not simply that husband and wife cleave to each other and are glued together. It goes beyond that: the two become one. God's math in marriage is that 1 + 1 does not equal 2, but 1.

This oneness is not purely physical and sexual. Undoubtedly that is part of what is meant here. Physical intimacy is an important part of the oneness of husband and wife, and indeed, sex is a beautiful, honorable thing in marriage. God has connected to it the great blessing of covenant children, but even aside from children it is a great blessing and joy that husband and wife can share in marriage. Within marriage it highlights the unity and companionship of one with another.

But physical intimacy is not the only thing that is meant by two becoming one. The oneness that God speaks of is more than just the body. And sexual oneness is not only something physical, but is also spiritual. In fact, if there is not more than physical oneness in marriage, the sexual relation loses all meaning.

The oneness of husband and wife is complete. There is a oneness of the whole of earthly life; the husband and wife share one life. There is a oneness of bodies and souls, of thinking and desiring, of hopes and disappointments, of labors and goals, of possessions and interests. So closely are they joined together that you cannot think about the one without the other. He cannot live without her, and she cannot live without him. He does not live for himself but for her, and she does not live for herself but for him.

The intimacy of the one-flesh union also says something about the pain of losing a spouse. The unique, inexpressible sorrow of the widow or widower indicates the intimacy of marriage. As one author put it, "They simply cannot describe their grief. How does one describe what it is to die in part, but still to go on living?"[1] So intimate is the mystery of God in marriage of taking two and making them one flesh!

What does this say about dating? Mostly something by contrast. The intimacy of marriage is only for marriage, and not for dating. Sexual intimacy has its place only in the safety and protection of the marriage bond. Likewise, emotional intimacy will grow during the time you date, but it is also something that only fully blossoms in marriage.

6. Marriage is God's work of joining a man and a woman.

Marriage is not the work of the man and the woman themselves, nor is it the work of the government or of the minister.

---

1   David J. Engelsma, *Marriage, the Mystery of Christ and the Church*, 3rd ed. (Jenison, MI: Reformed Free Publishing Association, 2014), 9.

Marriage is God's work. In Genesis 2, God did not put Adam to sleep, create the woman, and then set her free in the garden, hoping that she and Adam would eventually cross paths. Instead, God made the woman, woke Adam up, and then deliberately brought her to him. God was, as it were, the father of the bride, and he also acted to officiate the union of these two in marriage. Therefore, the Reformed marriage form points out that God "doth yet as with His hand bring unto every man his wife."[2]

What does this mean for dating? It means God is the one who so ordains the circumstances of our lives to bring to us our future spouse. It's interesting to hear stories of how he brings different couples together. One couple I know were friends for a long time before ever looking at one another romantically. Another couple started dating after a providential encounter in a hardware store. Although I don't recommend it, I know of another Christian couple who met via an online dating service. God has a different way for each one of us. Dating is done, therefore, with a trust in God to lead us to our husband or wife, to build and strengthen that relationship, and then to work on our wedding day to knit the two of us together into one.

---

2   Form for the Confirmation of Marriage before the Church, in *The Confessions and the Church Order of the Protestant Reformed Churches* (Grandville, MI: Protestant Reformed Churches in America, 2005), 306.

DISCUSSION QUESTIONS

1. Why are we talking about marriage already in chapter 2?

2. Is talking about marriage to the person you are dating difficult? If so, why?

3. Go back to the six truths about marriage that we learn from the first wedding. Think of some other ways that they apply to dating.

CHAPTER 3

WHEN SHOULD I START?

The first date. Those three words stir up a flood of nervous excitement. If you're a man, you're thinking about what you should wear. You're thinking about where you're going to take her and what you're going to do. You're thinking about picking her up and whether or not you are going to have to meet her parents. If you're a woman, you're thinking about what you're going to wear and how to do your hair and makeup. You're thinking about where he's going to take you. You're thinking about what you're going to talk about. You feel nervous and excited at the same time.

But before you knock on the door to see if she's ready and before you answer the door to let him in, stop and think: What brought you to this point? What decisions were made, whether consciously or unconsciously?

That's what I want to consider in this chapter. I want to challenge you to dig deep and examine some of the fundamental questions about dating. Specifically, I want to challenge you to examine why it is that you start dating in the first place. To my mind, there are three questions that have to be considered: Why do I want to date? When do I start dating? And who should take the lead?

THE MOTIVATION

The first thing that we must try to get a handle on is our motivation for dating. Ask yourself: Why is it that I want to date? Why do I want to go out with her? Why am I dating him?

There are a thousand wrong answers to those questions. If we're being honest with ourselves, we have to admit that these wrong motives are too often guiding our hearts.

One wrong reason why many young people date is that they want to have fun. I'm not saying that dating should not be fun; in many ways it will be very exciting. But for some, dating is only about having a good time. Dating is simply a means of entertainment. It's an excuse to have something to do on the weekends rather than sitting around at home.

Usually the "fun" that a person has in mind involves intimacy and the fulfillment of sexual desires. It's been said about young men that they think about sex every seven seconds. Whether true or not, the point in that statistic is that men think about sex. A lot. Sadly, this is often on their minds when they think about dating. To a certain extent, that's no less true of young women. They might not be thinking about sex specifically, but when they think about dating, they might have been led to think about emotional intimacy and romance. They might picture themselves in some fantasy world that they read about in a book or saw in their favorite romantic movie.

Another wrong reason why some people date is for their own sense of self-esteem. If they don't have a date to a social gathering, they feel undesirable or unwelcome. However, if they can always count on the presence and affection of another person, it gives them a sense of fulfillment, meaning, and value. It boosts their egos.

Others view dating as a game. Imagine this scenario. Emma is a godly, attractive young woman who has caught the attention of a group of male classmates. These young men make a wager among themselves to see who can be the first one to get her on a date. Unbeknownst to this poor girl, the young men aren't so much interested in dating her as they are in seeing which among them is the most attractive. They see dating as a way to jockey for social status.

Still others date simply out of a fear of being single for the rest of their lives. Perhaps this danger is more acute for those in their twenties or thirties. They see the prospect of remaining a lifelong single looming, and they can't imagine anything worse. Driven by desperation, they might foolishly throw themselves upon anyone who will have them, even if he or she is not a suitable spouse.

The one thing that all these wrong reasons for dating have in common is that they are all self-centered. If you strip them all down, what lies at the heart is selfishness and pride. The greatest danger is that I make dating about me, my happiness, my pleasure, my fulfillment, and my self-worth.

But this cannot be the motivation for dating. Dating driven by selfishness and pride is not distinctly Christian. That's dating like the world. That's dating done all wrong.

So, what should be our motivation? How ought we to answer the question, why do you want to date?

The proper motivation for dating is marriage. I spelled this out in more detail in the previous chapter, but it doesn't hurt to repeat it here: dating must be done with marriage in view. If marriage is the goal, then it must be in view from the very beginning.

Don't misunderstand this point. I'm not saying that you can only date a person if you are ready to marry him or her at that moment. That would be a gross overstatement. When you go on a first date with someone, you don't have to know that you're going to marry each other. But when you go on that date, you do have to be committed to the goal of marriage. You do have to go into it with a deliberate, serious mindset. When you knock on her door for the first time, you have to be consciously thinking, "The goal of this date tonight, and every other date, is marriage. I think that one day I might marry this person, and the goal is to see if that's possible."

The world laughs at this idea of dating with a view to marriage. They say that if you get too serious about marriage, you're going to miss out on all the fun. Go ahead and date, get to know one other, but don't be too serious about getting married.

The mature Christian won't be swayed by the attitude of the world. He or she will take dating seriously, committed to the ultimate goal of marriage. Remember, we date differently.

Closely related to the goal of marriage is the fact that our dating must be done to the glory of God. This is the ultimate motivation for the child of God in every aspect of his life. He worships with the people of God on the Sabbath, to the glory of God. He works hard the other six days of the week, to the glory of God. He handles his finances, to the glory of God. He eats and drinks, to the glory of God. This is the reason for our being created and the reason for our being saved. This is the motivation for all our life: God's glory.

In Isaiah 43:7 God says about each of his children, "I have created him for my glory." The inspired apostle Paul says in 1 Corinthians 10:31, "Whether therefore ye eat, or drink, or whatsoever ye do, do all to the glory of God." The Westminster Shorter Catechism, summarizing these passages, says memorably: "Man's chief end is to glorify God, and to enjoy him forever."[1]

---

1   Westminster Shorter Catechism Q&A 1, in Philip Schaff, ed., *The Creeds of Christendom with a History and Critical Notes*, 6th ed., 3 vols. (New York: Harper and Row, 1931; repr., Grand Rapids, MI: Baker Books, 2007), 3:676.

If our whole life is to be lived to God's glory, that means that we date and eventually marry with God's glory in view. But what does that mean? How does a person date to God's glory?

The answer is we date for marriage. When we date with marriage in view, we date to the glory of God. Marriage glorifies God. Marriage is a picture of God's gracious work of salvation, whereby he has drawn us into covenantal fellowship with him. Marriage is a symbol of Christ's relationship to his blood-bought church. Living together as husband and wife and reflecting that heavenly marriage brings glory to the God of our salvation. So when we date with marriage in view, we date to the glory of God.

The overarching desire in the heart of the Christian with respect to his dating is this: may God be glorified in all of my life, including in my dating!

THE TIMING

One of the questions we have to ask before we go on the first date is: when is the right time to start dating?

This is certainly a question that lives in the minds of your parents. As you get into your teenage years and start to show an interest in the opposite sex, the thought of you dating weighs heavily on your parents: When is the right time for them to let you start dating? Are you old enough?

Often the question of age does not even enter into the mind of a young person. Personally I can't remember as a teenager thinking, "When is the right time to start dating? Am I old enough?" I see that now as immaturity on my part. That question should have come up more, and I should have given it careful thought.

The guiding principle that we ought to follow in determining when to start dating is spiritual maturity. A young person ought not consider dating until he or she has reached a certain level of spiritual maturity. If marriage is the most important decision you will make, then it follows that you ought to be mature when making that decision. And if dating is for marriage, then dating should only be done by one who is spiritually mature.

This idea is understandably quite general. There is no way of objectively measuring one's spiritual maturity and readiness to date. Some have suggested that a helpful measure of spiritual maturity is public confession of faith in the church. This confession includes three promises, all of which give evidence of spiritual maturity:

- First, you promise that you understand and believe from the heart the biblical, Reformed faith.
- Second, you promise that you are committed to living a godly life.
- Third, you promise a commitment to church membership and submission to the officebearers in the church.

There is merit to the suggestion that once a young person has made public confession of faith, he or she is ready to start dating, although it is not a hard and fast rule. I'm content to leave the principle more general: date when you have reached a certain level of spiritual maturity.

Following from that general principle, my general advice—and it is just that, advice, since there is no direct command in God's word—is that you should be careful not to start dating too young. Again, it's hard to pinpoint a specific age. Some parents make a rule that their children can only date once they turn sixteen, and there may be some young people who are mature enough at sixteen to start dating. But I would venture to guess that most sixteen-year-olds are nowhere near the level of maturity necessary to start dating at that age. Some might not be mature enough to start dating even at twenty-one! Yet what you most often see today are fifteen- and sixteen-year-olds starting to pair off and go on dates.

If you are fifteen or sixteen and consider yourself ready to date, take a moment to stop and think about the future. If you start dating now and continue to date the same person, when you graduate from high school you will have dated for two or three years. Two or three years is a long time to date, enough time for you to know whether you can marry this person or not. Are you ready at eighteen, freshly graduated from high school, to get married? As a young man, are you going to be ready to support a wife and family? As a young woman, are you ready to be a wife and possibly a mother? Or do you have plans of going to college and getting a degree? If so, do you think that after three years of dating in high school you are willing to wait through four more years of college before getting married? Is that really wise?

Perhaps there are some of you who at sixteen are ready for all this. But as a general rule, most are not. If you are going to date, be sure that you are spiritually mature.

Some young people might object to this advice. One objection might be, "I'm not sure I'm ready to date, but there is a cute girl whom I'm interested in. If I don't claim her, someone else is going to do so." I understand the struggle and the risks that being patient carries. But if you are not ready to date, you simply shouldn't. Either God will direct the circumstances of both your lives so that you can date when you are both ready, or he will show that this was not the person he intended you to be with.

Closely related is the fact that when you start dating, you should be spiritually mature enough to be thinking about marriage. The motivation that we just mentioned should govern the timing. If you are not ready for marriage, then don't date. If you start to date but really aren't interested in marriage, you are doing a great disservice to the one you are dating. You are wasting his or her time with a relationship that is going nowhere. Be honest and fair to that person. If you aren't ready, don't date.

My advice to those who are too young is that they hold

off on dating. But I also have advice for those who are older. My advice to them is: start dating!

There is a danger that young people generally start dating at too young of an age. But there is also an increasing danger of older adults who do not date, who feel that they will never be ready for serious dating and so do not bother to gauge their spiritual maturity regarding finding a spouse. In fact, the general trend at present seems to be the desire to push off serious dating until a much later age.[2]

There may be differing reasons for this trend. Some might delay dating because they want to pursue higher education; they have set their sights not just on the four-year bachelor's degree, but also on a master's degree and a PhD. They don't have time to think about dating and marriage.

Others might delay dating because they think that it will hinder their ability to have fun. They don't want to be "burdened" with a boyfriend or girlfriend. They want life to be an endless party. They want to travel, see the world, and have adventures. They want to make a lot of money without having to worry about a spouse or children. So they push off serious dating until they are well into their twenties or even thirties.

---

2   According to one recent secular source, the average age of marriage has risen to twenty-nine for men and twenty-seven for women. See Kay Hymowitz, et al., *Knot Yet: The Benefits and Costs of Delayed Marriage in America* (The National Marriage Project at the University of Virginia, The National Campaign to Prevent Teen and Unplanned Pregnancy, and The Relate Institute, 2013), http://nationalmarriageproject.org/wp-content/uploads/2013/03/KnotYet-FinalForWeb.pdf.

I see this as a troubling trend. There may be some who don't go on a first date until they are older simply because God never brought someone into their path until then. Great! But for those who are deliberately putting off dating for selfish reasons, my advice is: stop being selfish, and start dating!

THE LEAD

A third question that we have to ask when we are considering dating is: who ought to take the lead?

Answer: the man.

We live in a society that preaches feminism and the equal authority of men and women. The women of the world are bold. They forcibly take the lead in a relationship and rule the relationship. They are in charge, and the men in their lives must meekly submit to their every beck and call.

But that isn't how things work in a Christian relationship. The man is the one who ought to take the lead. This goes back again to the marriage relationship and how it is a picture of Christ and his church. In that relationship, the church does not take the lead. She does not first choose and seek out Christ. Christ takes the lead. He chooses the church, seeks her out, and draws her to himself in an unbreakable bond. If Christ takes the lead in the heavenly marriage, then in our earthly relationships it makes sense that the man would take the lead. If the man is called to be the head or leader in marriage (Eph. 5:23), then he must take the lead in dating.

This truth means that it is the young man's responsibility to seek out the young woman in whom he is interested. It means that he is the one who initiates things and asks her out on a date. From then on, he takes the lead in the relationship.

This does not mean that the young woman has no voice and no part in the dating process at all. She certainly does. I like the way Cornelius Hanko put it: "This does not mean that she sits quietly at home waiting for a phone call for her first date. If my observations do not deceive me, most girls have the natural ability to attract the attention of the young man who interests them…[H]er winsome ways and pleasant smile can do much to attract the boy's attention."[3] Before dating, the young woman may certainly express her interest in the young man. Oftentimes, the young man needs all the help that he can get. He might be afraid to ask a girl out. He might be terrified about being rejected. The young woman can help with this, in subtle ways letting the young man know that she is interested.

But a godly woman does not want to take the lead in this relationship. She wants a young man to take the lead, even if she tends to be the more "take-charge" type. After all, she is looking for a husband who will be her spiritual head and leader one day. She wants him to show that he's capable of this already from the beginning, with just the small step of initiating their relationship.

---

3   Cornelius Hanko, *Leaving Father and Mother: Biblical Courtship and Marriage* (Grandville, MI: Reformed Free Publishing Association, 2001).

I fear that even in the church there are too many young men who refuse to take this step, to take the lead. Too often I hear stories of spiritually minded young women who have a desire to be married but are never asked out on a date. In the church sits a swarm of young men who are also single, yet have never plucked up the courage to ask anyone out. Young men, wake up! Get out there and ask these young women on a date. So what if you get shot down a time or two? The young women of the church are pleading with you to take the lead. From time to time I have the foolish thought of taking the young men and young women, lining them against opposite walls, numbering them off, and sending them off in pairs to go on a date.[4] I know, it's not realistic. But I hope for anything that might encourage a young man to take the lead in pursuing a godly young woman and initiating that first date.

In turn, ladies, if a young man asks you out, unless you are certain you cannot date him, don't hesitate to give him a shot.

---

4   Elisabeth Elliot has made a similar point. See Kevin DeYoung, *Just Do Something: A Liberating Approach to Finding God's Will* (Chicago: Moody Publishers, 2009), 108.

DISCUSSION QUESTIONS

1. What are your motivations for dating?

2. Have your parents set an age limit for when you may start dating? Why might they have done that?

3. In what ways ought the man to take the lead in dating? Why is this important?

4. If the man leads, what does that mean for the woman? What role does she play?

CHAPTER 4

WHO'S THE ONE?

I n many ways this chapter gets right to the heart of Christian dating. What I write here is devoted to helping answer the question, "Whom should I be dating? What do I look for in a boyfriend or girlfriend?" Once you've answered the questions raised in the previous chapter—why do you want to date? are you ready to date?—then you're ready to ask yourself the next question: "Who's the one?"

I'm not sure it's possible to overstate the importance of this question and its answer. What makes marriage the most important decision you might ever make is that you are going to be living with that person for the rest of your life. You'd better be quite sure before you enter into the lifelong bond of marriage that you know exactly the kind of person you are marrying.

What follows are four guidelines to think through carefully as you begin to look for someone to date.

The very idea of setting forth rules and guidelines to follow in choosing a boyfriend or girlfriend is laughable to the world. The world preaches that you can date and love and marry whomever you want, no questions asked. Unbelieving parents cross their fingers and hope their child dates and marries well, but they have little to offer in the way of guidance or advice.

But remember, the Christian dates differently. The child of God realizes that he may not date and marry anyone he likes. The word of God guides and limits his choice of a future spouse.

OPPOSITE SEX

The first principle of God's word for whom to date is that he or she must be someone of the opposite sex. This is not the place to give a detailed explanation of the pertinent biblical texts, but there are many (see Lev. 18:22; 20:13; Rom. 1:26–27; 1 Cor. 6:9–10; 1 Tim. 1:8–11).[1]

This point might seem so obvious to the child of God that it hardly feels necessary to mention except in passing. However, it is a point that has to be made. The reason why it's necessary is that we are living in a society that encourages

---

1   For an explanation of these passages, see Kevin DeYoung, *What Does the Bible Really Teach about Homosexuality?* (Wheaton, IL: Crossway, 2015), 25–67; or Sam Allberry, *Is God Anti-Gay?* (London: The Good Book Company, 2015), 25–38.

same-sex relationships. It's becoming increasingly normal for junior high and high school students to "come out" as gay or lesbian, which the world hails as progress.[2] Those who express their romantic interest in the same sex are heralded as heroes. We all supposedly need the courage to express our true selves, live as we please, and choose what makes us happy. Anyone who discourages this is an ignorant, closed-minded bigot.

Sadly, with the increase of this wickedness in the world, there is also an increase in the number of Christians who struggle with same-sex attraction. Many believing young people are deeply confused about their sexual desires. For some, all they can ever remember is having an attraction toward those of the same sex.

The answer to this confusion is not to encourage these troubled Christians to follow their desires. The answer is not to listen to yourself and do whatever feels natural. To give this advice would be to create even more trouble.

The answer is, first, boldly to declare the doctrine of indwelling sin. Our natures are so corrupt that a child of God may well grow up knowing only an attraction to the same sex. But this attraction is not "normal"; this is due to the fall into sin.

The answer is, second, boldly to declare the gospel. There is in Christ forgiveness of these sinful desires of the penitent

---

2   For proof, see the highly influential special issue of *National Geographic* on "Gender Revolution" (January 2017).

believer as well as the power to fight against them (see 1 Cor. 6:9–11).

Third, the answer is boldly to declare the truth of God concerning sexuality and marriage. In the beginning God distinguished the human race between male and female. He designed marriage to be a one-flesh union between one man and one woman for life. Therefore, the Christian in his dating seeks out one of the opposite sex. If the troubled young person finds this difficult, the only alternative is to remain single and chaste. No other option exists.

BELIEVER

The second principle of God's word for whom to date is that he or she must be a believing child of God.

The Bible is unmistakably clear on this matter. In Genesis 26:34–35 we read of the heartbreak of Isaac and Rebekah when their son Esau married two unbelieving wives. It wasn't just the fact that he married two wives that grieved them, but it was the fact that they were also ungodly that was such a sorrow.

Throughout the history of the Old Testament there are repeated warnings against allowing the sons of God to marry the daughters of Belial (see Judges 3:6). This history also tells of the terrible consequences when they did.

Amos 3:3 says, "Can two walk together, except they be agreed?" This applies more broadly than to marriage, but it certainly has application to marriage as well. Two cannot walk together in the closest possible earthly relationship if they are not in fundamental spiritual agreement.

First Corinthians 7:39 says of the widow that she is free to marry whom she desires, so long as it is in the Lord. This applies generally to all dating and marrying: it must be in the Lord, that is, between two believers who are both united by faith to Christ Jesus.

Second Corinthians 6:14–18 exhorts the child of God not to be unequally yoked to an unbeliever. Again, this has application to all of our relationships, but what yoke is stronger than marriage? In marriage also it is necessary that we not be yoked to an unbeliever.

Many in the Reformed faith trace their origins to the Netherlands. The Dutch understood this principle. A common phrase once was, "*Twee geloven op een kussen, daar slaapt de duivel tussen*": "Where there are two faiths on one pillow, the devil sleeps between them there." The point is that where there is a marriage between two who are not of the same faith, the devil is working hard to sow seeds of division.

There are some who think that when they date an unbeliever, they will influence him or her to become a believer. God does say that the believing wife may be able to influence an unbelieving husband (1 Pet. 3:1–2). But that was addressing a situation where the wife was also an unbeliever at the time of the wedding and was later converted. We must not try to be wiser than God, who clearly states in his word that we are not to date and marry an unbeliever. What often happens is that the believer is influenced by the unbeliever, and not the unbeliever by the believer. Marriage is not a mission field. Dating is not evangelism. We may not date an unbeliever.

This raises a related question: Is it permissible to date someone who is a Christian but who belongs to a different denomination of churches? For example, may a member of the Protestant Reformed Churches date someone who belongs to the United Reformed Church? Or the Christian Reformed Church? Or a Baptist congregation?

The short answer is: Yes, but with some conditions.

Yes, you may date someone who belongs to another denomination so long as that one shows him- or herself to be a believer.

Yes, you may date someone who belongs to another denomination so long as there is a fundamental agreement in faith and spiritual life.

Yes, you may date someone who belongs to another denomination so long as there is a willingness to openly discuss and work through any doctrinal and practical differences that exist.

Yes, you may date someone who belongs to another denomination so long as there is an understanding that your membership in a church of Christ that most faithfully holds to the marks of a true church is non-negotiable.

There are many strong Christian couples who have grown

up in different denominations. However, real doctrinal and practical differences still exist in these relationships. To think that these things won't affect a marriage is foolish in the extreme. These things do matter and have to be taken into consideration.

These differences have to be discussed. A relationship where these things are not discussed and worked through is not healthy and should be ended. Additionally, you must deal with these differences early on, before a strong emotional connection is formed. The fundamental unity in marriage is a spiritual oneness.

Too often it happens that a young man and young woman from different church backgrounds start to date. They don't talk about their differences. ("It's not so urgent, right? We'll have all the time in the world later to figure it out.") But what happens is that they form a deep emotional connection with each other. Then, when the differences do finally come up and they realize that there isn't spiritual unity there, they cannot break off the relationship. Their emotions have run too far ahead.

Let me end this section with a positive encouragement: start looking for a spouse in your church and denomination and in the good Christian school you attend (if you have one). Not everyone will find their spouse there. Not everyone in your church and school is right to date. But this is the best place to start looking. In these places, there exists already a level of spiritual oneness.

MATURE

The third principle of God's word for whom to date is that he or she must reveal a level of spiritual maturity.

If we are thinking about dating as we should, then we are dating with a view ultimately to marriage. It is so essential in marriage that we be married to one who not only confesses to be a Christian but shows that he or she is a mature and godly Christian.

This does not mean that you may only date and marry one who has reached the pinnacle of spiritual development. This is unrealistic. If that were a condition for marriage, we would all remain single. Allowance has to be made for a person growing and maturing over time. Even if you marry someone who is spiritually mature, you will realize over the years that he or she is more mature now than on the day of your wedding.

Still, we may not settle for less here. We should seek out and date only one who shows him- or herself to be spiritually mature.

Let's consider what that looks like for young men, for young women, and then for both.

1. For him

What qualities should a young woman be looking for in a young man?

The serious-minded young woman has her eye on marriage and therefore is looking for a young man who will one day be her husband. This means that the dateable young man is going to give evidence of the qualities God requires in a husband.

The Reformed marriage form is helpful in setting forth the main biblical requirements of the husband.[3] They can be easily remembered as the three L's.

First, the Christian husband is called to *lead* his wife (see Eph. 5:23). His leadership of her is especially important from a spiritual point of view. He ultimately bears the responsibility before God for the spiritual growth not only of himself, but also of his wife, and he takes this seriously.

This means that the mature young man will show himself already in dating to be a leader. He does not yet lead as if he is the husband of his future wife. He recognizes she is still under the authority of her father until they are married. But he gives evidence in dating that he can be a strong leader one day, especially when it comes to spiritual matters. He initiates spiritual conversations. He expresses interest in praying together and having devotions. He desires to go to church together and to talk about the sermon. He reads good books and magazines and is eager to share what he is learning with his girlfriend. He takes the lead in setting and maintaining sexual boundaries.

Second, the Christian husband is called to *love* his wife (see Eph. 5:25). His leadership of his wife is characterized

---

3 Form for the Confirmation of Marriage before the Church, in *Confessions and Church Order*, 307.

by love. The way in which he shows his love is by giving of himself for his wife. Just as Christ's love for his church was manifest in his giving of himself to the death of the cross, so the groom shows his love for his bride by giving of himself for her.

This must be evident in the young man you are interested in dating. He does not try to seduce his girlfriend by whispering in her ear that he loves her and then leading her into sexual sin. His love is holy and pure and desires to preserve the purity of his future wife. He shows he loves her by giving of himself and willingly sacrificing on her behalf.

The dateable young man is not, therefore, a domineering brute. Young women should be very leery of young men who abuse the idea of headship and authority. A young woman should be on the lookout for any signs that a young man is prone to belittling her, controlling her, losing his temper easily toward her, and abusing her. These things indicate the young man is not loving and is not a suitable husband.[4]

Third, the Christian husband is called to *labor* to provide for his wife (see Gen. 3:17–19). He works hard by the sweat of his brow from day to day to provide for the physical needs of the home and to be able to give to the church and the poor.

---

4   For more on the signs of an abusive boyfriend, read the section "Early Warning Signs" in Lundy Bancroft, *Why Does He Do That?: Inside the Minds of Angry and Controlling Men* (New York: Berkley Books, 2002), 114–23. Bancroft does not write from a Christian viewpoint, but his book is very helpful.

It's important in dating that the young man give evidence of his willingness to work hard. It ought to be very concerning to the young woman (as I'm sure it is to her parents) when a young man shows himself to be lazy. Perhaps he spends all his time playing video games or playing sports or having a good time with his friends and is loathe to work hard. If he is serious about marriage and a mature man, then he is ready to put those things away and take responsibility for his work.

Dating my wife brought this point home for me. Her father owned a number of rental properties in downtown Grand Rapids, MI, which were constantly in need of repairs and cleaning and a fresh coat of paint. The joke was that one of the "stipulations" for dating any of his daughters was that we suitors be willing to spend Saturdays helping at the rental houses. His point was a good one. He was making sure we were willing to work hard to provide for his daughters.

This raises the question of a young man who is going to college to earn a degree while dating seriously. Should he only marry when he has graduated? Should he drop out if he decides to get married? There are no hard and fast rules here. I can only speak from my own experience. My wife and I got married when I was finished with two years of college. I still had two more years to go and then four years of post-graduate studies. We simply made it work. I worked part-time jobs while going to school, and my wife supplemented our income by working out of the home. And we were generously supported by family and the church. I would say that if a man is going to school to get a good job and shows that he is a hard worker, there is no reason to delay marriage because he is still in school.

In summary, the dateable young man must be of the highest spiritual character. Song of Solomon 1:3 says, "Because of the savour of thy good ointments thy name is as ointment poured forth, therefore do the virgins love thee." The point here is that as much as a woman is attracted by the sweet-smelling cologne of a man, she is most attracted by his good name and character. Far more important than his rippling biceps, six-pack abs, expensive car, and dashing good looks is his spiritual character.

2. For her

On the flip side, what qualities should a young man be looking for in a young woman?

The serious-minded young man has his eye on marriage and therefore is looking for a young woman who will one day be his wife. This means that the dateable young woman is going to give evidence of the qualities God requires in a wife.

The first calling that the Bible gives to the wife in marriage is to be a help to her husband (see Gen. 2:18, 20). She views herself as her husband's complement, and she strives to help him in every way possible. She encourages his leadership, rejoices in his love, and supports him as he labors.

So also ought the Christian young woman to show herself to be a willing helper. She is not vain and self-centered. She is not materialistic or lazy. But she has a servant's heart. She is willing to give of herself for others. She is willing to be inconvenienced as she seeks the well-being of another.

The related calling of the wife in marriage is to reverence her husband and submit to his authority (see Eph. 5:22–24, 33). She does not rebel or try to live independently of him, but she acknowledges his authority as being from God, and she willingly places herself under his leadership. Her submission is the specific form that her love for her husband takes (Titus 2:4).

This quality must be found in the dateable young woman. Being under the authority still of her father, she does not submit to her boyfriend. But she should give evidence of being ready to do this one day when they are married. She is not rebellious. She does not relish living independently and being her own authority. She reveals that she is clothed with the inner beauty of a "meek and quiet spirit" (1 Pet. 3:4).

Her submissive spirit does not now or in marriage make her a doormat or wallflower. It doesn't mean that she has no gifts or no opinion. She does have gifts, and she uses them. She does have an opinion, and she is free to express it. But she is ready to place all these things into the service of her marriage and home.

You'll notice, young men, that I didn't mention anything about her physical beauty or her ability to cook and clean.

If you find a woman who has these qualities along with the spiritual qualities, then give thanks to God. But these are not the most essential things. What might catch your eye at first is her good looks, but what ought to keep your interest is her inner, spiritual beauty (Prov. 31:30).

3. For both

In addition to the things mentioned above specifically for men and women, there are some other qualities that must characterize both sexes. The following is by no means exhaustive, but I mention some of the more important ones.

Both must walk closely with God. The strength of your marriage is your spiritual oneness in the Lord, so it is important for both to be walking closely with him. This will show itself in a commitment to regular intake of God's word, frequent prayer, and love for the church and her worship. Someone once said, "Run hard toward Christ. Then, look around you for a spouse who's running hard in the same direction."

Both must be trustworthy (Prov. 31:11) and honest (Eph. 4:25). Warning bells ought to go off if the person you're dating gives evidence of lying and manipulation. You simply cannot have a strong relationship with another person without trust and honesty.

Both must be selfless (Phil. 2:3–4). There is no room in a healthy marriage for selfishness. In a strong marriage, husband is thinking about wife, and wife is thinking about husband. Already in your dating show yourself to be selfless and willing to serve.

Both must show themselves ready to confess their faults (Prov. 28:13) and to forgive (Col. 3:13). No one is perfect, even if they might seem that way at first. The more you get to know someone, the more you will see his or her faults. The important thing is not finding a person without faults, but finding someone who humbly confesses those faults and forgives you when you show your faults.

Both must be committed to growing (2 Pet. 3:18) and changing. The important thing is not so much where you've been or where you are currently, but in what direction you are heading. In a healthy relationship both are headed in the direction of greater maturity.

While it's essential that we look for one to date who is a mature believer, it's good to remember that no one is perfect. Our standards must not be too low, but neither may they be unrealistically high. The fact of the matter is that even the mature believer has room for growth. Remember this too: you've got a lot of room for growth yourself!

ATTRACTION

If we have followed the previous three steps, we have whittled the field of potential mates down to those of the opposite sex who are believers and spiritually mature. But this does not yet lead us to one individual. The pool is smaller, but it still includes a large number of people. The fourth principle of

God's word for whom to date, then, is that we are to trust the Lord's hand to guide through our life circumstances.

There is a sense in which the child of God should look at every single believer of the opposite sex as a potential mate. Sometimes we can get wrongly hung up on waiting for "the one" or our "soul mate." A person might be constantly anxious about missing out on the one person he or she is to marry. But this anxiety is unnecessary. I realize this is a bit of an over-exaggeration, but I'm almost tempted to say that a mature believing man ought to be able to marry any mature believing woman. (Almost.)

If we have followed the other principles, then we trust in God to lead us to the person of his choosing through the various circumstances of our lives. Ultimately he is the one who will direct our path to intersect with the path of our future spouse. His hand brings to every man his wife, and to every wife her husband.

One of the ways that God does lead us to our spouse is through attraction. This is a difficult emotion to define, but it involves God causing one soul to be drawn to the soul of another. There are three aspects to attraction: physical, emotional, and spiritual.

I mention *physical* attraction first not because it is the most important. In fact, it is the least important. I mention it first because it is often the first thing that draws one person to another, especially a man to a woman. Often the physical attraction brings two people together, but it is the other things that keep them together. We must not think that physical attraction, or even a healthy concern for one's own physical appearance, is inherently sinful. It certainly is sinful for a person to date another only on the basis of looks and sexual lust. But the physical attraction between two Christians is not inherently wrong.

There is also an *emotional* attraction between a man and woman. They are drawn to one another's personality. This is more important than the physical. A person might be physically attractive, but their personality might be unattractive. A person who is physically less attractive might have a more attractive personality. Some say that opposites attract, and certainly this is true for some. The extroverted man might be drawn to the introverted woman. The frugal woman might be drawn to the generous man. But this is not a hard and fast rule. Sometimes those who are very much alike are drawn to each other. Every person might be drawn to different things.

Then there is the *spiritual* attraction. Of all things this is the most important, more important than the physical and the emotional. You might be initially drawn to a person by looks and personality, but the thing that ought to hold you together for life is the strength of the spiritual connection that you have in Christ.

Through these means, the Lord will lead us to the person whom he has eternally determined for us to marry.

The world makes much of finding someone with whom you are compatible. By that they mean they want to date someone who meets their qualifications, who pleases them, and who will allow them to continue to do what they want without changing. But for the Christian, although we must be careful whom we date, our concern is not with the other person meeting a long list of qualifications. The focus is less on finding the right one and more on ourselves becoming the kind of mature believer that a fellow believer would want to date. We should give more thought to *becoming* someone rather than *finding* someone.

DISCUSSION QUESTIONS

1. What things ought we to keep in mind when considering whom to date?

2. How are we to handle a situation where we are interested in dating someone who is not a Christian? What about someone who belongs to a different denomination? See if you can find parents, friends, teachers, or fellow church members whose spouses did not originally belong to a Reformed denomination. How did these people approach dating outside their church? Do they wish they had done so differently? What advice would they share with you?

3. What things ought to characterize the spiritually mature man?

4. What things ought to characterize the spiritually mature woman?

5. Place the following in order of importance to you in looking for one to date: physical, emotional, spiritual attraction. Is your order proper?

CHAPTER 5

WHAT'S THERE TO DO ON DATES?

Sara is pacing nervously in her parents' living room. Joel is supposed to stop by at 6:00 to pick her up for a date. He shows up on time, rings the doorbell, and talks for a few minutes to her parents. When Sara is in the other room looking for her shoes, her dad, trying to appear nonchalant, asks Joel, "So, what do you guys have planned for tonight?"

Joel responds, "Uh…we're going to…um…I'm not sure. I was going to see what Sara wanted to do."

Dad is clearly not impressed. "Mmm…be sure to have her home on time."

Sara is finally ready to go. After saying goodbye, they get

in Joel's car, and as they are pulling out of the driveway he asks, "So, what do you want to do tonight?"

Sara's stomach flips. "I don't care. Whatever you had planned."

"Well, I really didn't have anything planned," Joel admits sheepishly. "I was just going to see what you wanted to do."

Sara pauses and then takes charge. "Why don't we…"

Does this exchange sound familiar? Have you ever found yourself in a similar situation? Sadly, I can relate. I look back on the years of dating my wife and remember many times when I went into a date with little forethought, and I fear that I'm not unique in this regard. Too often dating is done with a fly-by-the-seat-of-your-pants, we'll-make-this-up-as-we-go mentality.

For that reason, a chapter devoted to what to do in dating is important. In this chapter you'll look at some of the principles that guide the Christian's activities on dates and also find some practical advice on what to do on a date.

DATING VERSUS COURTSHIP

I think this is the best place to deal with a question that Christian young people and their parents regularly ask: "Is it okay to date? Or is courtship the best way to go?"

Before answering that question, let's understand what is meant by these two things. When we talk about dating, we usually have in mind a young man and a young woman getting to know one another by going off and doing different activities on their own. There is often the expectation of a certain level of physical contact, such as holding hands, hugging, and kissing.

On the other hand, when most people think about courtship, they think about an old-fashioned, Victorian way of life. Perhaps they imagine the way their grandparents met and got married. Usually courtship involves the close supervision of parents over the young man and young woman. They do not go off on their own to do activities but spend most of their time in the fellowship of family and friends. They may have some time alone, but that time is very limited and structured. Also, with courtship there are usually strict limitations on the amount of physical contact the two can have. Holding hands might be acceptable, or hugs might be always from the side, never from the front. Kissing is usually not permitted, so that the two share their first kiss on the day of their wedding.

Generally speaking, the differences can be summarized as follows:

	Christian Dating	Christian Courtship
Parental pre-approval?	Father's advice, but not prior approval.	Father's prior approval.
Parental supervision?	Supervision is not constant.	Close supervision and chaperoning.
Physical contact?	More physical contact allowed.	Little or no physical contact allowed.
Who initiates?	The man ought to, but the woman may (e.g., Ruth).	Only the man may initiate.

So, which is best?

There are strong opinions on both sides. Proponents of dating are often quite scornful of courtship as something that is outdated and unrealistic. More moderate critics of courtship point out that it can inhibit someone from ever getting married, often because no one is ever good enough for "Daddy's princess." On the other side, those who are in favor of courting are often vehement in their denunciation of dating as worldly and inherently sinful.

I hope here to avoid both extremes. Contrary to outspoken supporters of courtship, I do not believe that dating is wrong. In fact, I think it is preferable. The Bible gives certain principles that govern our behavior as we look for one to marry, but it does not prescribe a certain form. From a practical point of view, I do believe that dating provides the best opportunity for a young man and young woman to learn about one another.

That being said, I see many qualities of courtship that ought to be incorporated as a necessary corrective in our dating. The attitude that a young man and young woman are always alone in their dating needs to be corrected by spending more time with family and friends. The attitude that a young man and young woman can have a great deal of physical contact ought to be more strictly limited.

I see things in both methods that are worth our consideration, though I realize this answer might not satisfy those on either extreme of the dating/courtship debate. Call it whatever you want: dating, courting, or some dating/courting hybrid. (I call it dating.) But in the end it doesn't matter much what you call it, so long as you are intentional about what happens in it.

LET'S GET TO KNOW EACH OTHER

One of the advantages of dating is that it provides the opportunity for a young man and a young woman to get to know each other well. I see this as the primary objective in dating. As I've been hammering home, the goal of dating is marriage. And if you're going to marry that person, you have to know that he or she is a suitable spouse. The conviction that this person is the right one for you to marry comes only through taking the time to get to know each other.

This means that the majority of your time together ought to be spent talking. To put it a bit crassly, if the one you are dating wants to use his or her mouth for kissing more than for talking, you'd better look for someone else.

The only way for two people to get to know one another is by sharing their thoughts and values and opinions with each other. If you stop and think for a moment, you'll realize that there is no shortage of topics to talk about. For example, you certainly want to talk to one another about your day, about your work, about things that happened recently, about your interests, about your struggles, and about your dreams. You want to find out what kind of man he is and what kind of woman she is. Is he going to be a loving husband? Will she be a submissive wife? Before you get married you also need to talk about such things as your view of marriage and divorce, the callings of the husband and wife, the specific expectations and roles of each, the desire for children, a mother working outside the home, the details of childrearing, schooling of children, how to handle finances, and church membership. You don't have to talk about these things on the first date, but at some point you will have to explore all these subjects together.

As you talk through these different subjects, you will come to see how close you are in your thinking, and you will also see areas of difference. Don't be surprised by this. Sometimes a couple might date for a few months and think that they are in agreement on everything. But inevitably, they will disagree about something, at which point it might seem like their perfect world is crashing down around them. Again, don't be too shocked when this happens, and don't immediately conclude that you are not meant for each other. It's common for two people who grew up in different families to disagree on certain things. Be open and honest. Work through the differences together. If the difference is over something major and you can't reach an agreement, then you may need to break up. But first try to work through it and come to an agreement.

This is good preparation for marriage. When you are married, you are going to learn more about your spouse than you could have in dating, and you will have times when you disagree. Then there is not the option of walking away, so you must work through it together.

It's especially important that you come to learn about one another spiritually. This sets our dating apart from the dating of the world. Ask one another about your relationship to the Lord. Talk freely about spiritual things. Go to church together and spend time afterward discussing what things you found especially applicable in the sermon. Take time to have devotions together. Especially take time to pray together. This is probably going to be hard for the young man, but it is important that his future wife see him lead in this way and hear him pray. This is an area that I look back on with regret. I remember a few times praying with my wife while we were dating, but it was not very often. I wish now that I would have taken the lead in this respect, as I should have. I'd encourage you to take a few minutes at the end of every date to pray for one another and for your relationship. This not only ends the date on a spiritual note, but it also helps guard against sexual temptations that might arise at that time. If you are praying together, you're probably not going to feel comfortable pushing the sexual boundaries.

As healthy as it is to share, I think I must also include a warning about over-sharing, especially early on. Believe it or not, I grew up and dated in the days prior to texting and social media. But I've heard from some young people that those who are dating nowadays tend to over-share. They text one another daily, often relaying the most mundane of details about their lives, such as what they are wearing or what they ate for lunch. The trouble is that when they find themselves on a date, they don't know what to talk about. No information is new because they've already shared everything. Especially in the first months and even years of dating, limit this kind of contact. Leave things to be shared in person. Preserve some sense of "mystery" so that the one you are dating wants to learn more.

Another danger is that you might do all the talking and never listen to your date. This is a danger for both the young men and the young women. By nature we are conceited and interested only in ourselves. So we talk and talk and talk. We talk about our dreams, or things we've done, or what upsets us, and we never get around to learning about the other person. A good communicator is someone who knows when to be quiet and listen. James 1:19 says, "Let every man be swift to hear, slow to speak." Ask questions of the other person, and then close your mouth and listen carefully with a genuine interest in what he or she is saying.

It's also worth pointing out that the purpose in getting to know one another is that you get to know each other as you truly are. On the first few dates you are probably going to put your best foot forward. You are going to be the perfect gentleman and perfect lady. And that's good. But over time you need to know who the other person really is. You can't put on airs and pretend to be someone you're not. As frightening as it may seem, you want to know not only the other person's strengths, but also his or her weaknesses, and you want them to know your weaknesses too. You must not fear to expose your true self in the always messy and dangerous business of love.

I am convinced that this means sharing some of the deepest and darkest secrets we keep with our future spouse. If you struggle with pornography, you have to tell your girlfriend. If you have given away your virginity, you have to tell your boyfriend. If you have been physically or sexually abused, you have to tell the one you are going to marry. I don't believe that in every situation you have to tell them all the details. But you do have to tell them the truth. Again, these struggles and personal temptations are definitely not something to share on the first date. But at some point, perhaps when you are engaged, you owe it to your future spouse to bring them up. Too many spouses have been hurt when, years after getting married, they find out about secrets that deeply affected their husband or wife prior to marriage. These things have affected marriages in significant ways, though the other spouse might never have known why. That's not fair to them. They have a right to know these things about the one they are going to marry.

The general guideline for what to do in dating is this: let everything revolve around getting to know one another better.

A MAN WITH A PLAN

In this section I want to give some practical advice for what to do on dates.

One of the keys is to go into a date with a plan. This is something that I recall my mom saying often and, as I mentioned earlier, one of the weak areas in my own dating. Have a pretty clear idea of what you are going to do. Make sure you know how to get there. Have some idea of the amount of time it takes to get there and how much time is needed for the activity you are planning so that you and your date can be home on time.

This advice applies particularly to the young men. This isn't to say that the young women can't have a hand in the planning of dates; they certainly can. But the young men ought to take the lead here. If you are going to be the leader and chief decision-maker later in your marriage, start preparing for that now by planning the dates. This is something that most young women want. To them it conveys the idea that you were thinking about the date beforehand and are excited about it. They want to see that you are emotionally invested. Nothing hurts more than for a young woman to have the feeling that you just showed up without any real excitement or forethought.

Not only does your planning of the date impress your girlfriend, it also says something to your future in-laws. They are going to be nervous if you are taking their daughter out without knowing where she is going. On the flip side, if you have a plan, they are going to see that you are a mature young man and be glad you are dating their daughter. They want to know she is in good hands. Give them that confidence by being a man with a plan.

When you plan a date, try to be creative. Don't do the same things over and over, week after week. It's too easy to get stuck in a rut and always visit the same restaurant and do the same activities. Think outside of the box and do things outside of your comfort zone. Ask other young couples for ideas of what they have done on dates. If something is a flop, have a good laugh about it together and then try something different next time. Remember to do things that the other person likes. Don't pick activities that you are interested in, but think about what might interest the one you are dating.

Even though I'm encouraging you to date with a plan, this does not mean that you have to spend a lot of money. Having a plan of doing something is going to require some money on your part, but the fact that you are willing to spend money on your date shows that you care about her and are genuinely interested in the relationship. However, it does not help to spend ridiculous amounts of money doing all sorts of wild and extravagant activities. It's going to be quite a letdown if you spend your dating years on fancy yachts and expensive restaurants, only to get married and live in a tiny apartment on a shoestring budget. The point is not to impress your date with your money, but to create opportunities to get to know one another as you truly are. So think ahead, spend some money, but don't feel like every date has to be over the top.

Though the suggestions here are practical, dating in this way bodes well for future married life. Planning ahead, being creative, thinking about the other person first, and being a good steward of finances are all desirable qualities in marriage.

I want to conclude this chapter by giving some examples of what you could do together on dates. This list is certainly not exhaustive. But I hope it gives you some idea of the different activities available to a young couple. I know that if I was still dating, a list like this would be helpful in planning a date.

- Attend church and school functions (church picnics, Bible studies, special lectures, church league softball games, family fun nights, choir and band concerts).
- Go out for breakfast, lunch, brunch, or just dessert. You don't always have to go out for supper and have dates at night. Consider going out for breakfast on a Saturday morning and spending a few hours together.
- Work or serve together (paint a room, rake leaves, shovel snow, babysit nephews and nieces).
- Go for a walk through a nice park.
- Go hiking through a forest, by a mountain, along a lakeshore.
- Grab a couple of poles and a can of worms and go fishing.
- Borrow some bikes and go for a bike ride.
- Visit a farmers market, an orchard, or a greenhouse.
- Visit elderly grandparents.

- Host a game night with family or friends.
- Go skiing or snowboarding. The ski lift makes a nice, quiet place to talk.
- Borrow a couple of four-wheelers and ride some trails.
- Take in a museum, an art gallery, or the performance of a symphony orchestra.
- Play a round of golf, a tennis match, or go bowling.
- Go rummaging, hit up garage sales, or search for antiques.
- Watch your local minor league baseball or hockey team or your local college basketball team.
- Get some friends and go on a double date or group date.
- Make supper together.
- Once a year get dressed up and go for a fancy dinner somewhere.

Remember, be creative. Get ideas from others. Make a plan. Get to know one another. Have fun!

DISCUSSION QUESTIONS

1. What is the difference between dating and courtship?

2. Evaluate yourself: Do you tend to dominate conversations? Or are you a good listener? Explain how this affects dating.

3. How much contact via texting or social media is appropriate while dating?

4. What other things can you think of to do on a date? Add five things to the list at the end of this chapter.

CHAPTER 6

WHAT'S THE PLACE OF MY PARENTS AND OTHERS?

At first glance, this might seem like a strange subject to include in a book on dating. Maybe you're thinking, "What do my parents have to do with my dating?" Certainly that's the attitude of the youth of the world. In their minds this chapter could be written very briefly: my parents don't have any say in who I date or what I do in dating, and they'd better stay out of it.

But the attitude of the Reformed young man or woman must be different. We recognize that God has placed our parents in a position of authority over us. That authority includes their good instruction and wise guidance in all areas of life, including our dating. The amount of oversight our parents exercise will depend on our age and whether or not we are still living under their roof, but our attitude is one of respect and reverence toward them and a submission to their authority over us.

THE EXAMPLE OF ABRAHAM

One of the best ways to see the authority of parents in this sphere of life is through the example of Abraham in Genesis 24.

Abraham was concerned about his son Isaac. Isaac was forty years old and showing no initiative in finding a wife for himself. This was characteristic of Isaac. Whereas his father Abraham and his future son Jacob were unafraid to take the initiative and even attempt to run ahead of God, Isaac was slow to act. The reason Abraham was concerned about Isaac's failure to look for a wife was the covenantal promise of God to give him as many children as the stars in the sky (Gen. 15:4–5). If Isaac didn't find a wife and have children, Abraham's line would die off.

Abraham turned for help to his chief servant. He made the servant swear that he would not get a wife for Isaac from among the heathen women of Canaan but that he would look for a wife among Abraham's relatives in Haran. The servant made the long journey to Haran, and when he arrived, he prayed that God would lead him to the wife for Isaac. No sooner had he finished praying than beautiful Rebekah appeared. She took the servant to her family's home, and there the servant told his story. When he was finished,

Rebekah agreed to go back with him immediately to be the wife of Isaac.

When the servant finally returned with Rebekah, Isaac was out in the field. He saw her, loved her, and immediately they were married.

The point of this history is not to say that all parents have to arrange the marriages of their children (although some parents might wish to!). But the main takeaway is that parents are to be involved in the process of who their children marry. Their God-given authority means they have a say in the dating of their children.

THE ROLE OF PARENTS

What exactly is the role of your parents in your dating and marrying?

Their role began early on, even before you were old enough to date. While you were still young they instructed you already about dating and marriage. They might have taken the opportunity of a sermon on Sunday or a passage read in family devotions to warn you against sin and to give positive instruction on marriage. They taught you the proper way that a man treats a woman and the proper way for a woman to respond to a man.

One of the most powerful ways in which they influenced you was by the example of their own marriage. If their marriage was a mess, it probably does not matter how good the instruction they gave was. As children you learned more from the example of dad being unloving or mom being unsubmissive. But if your parents' marriage was strong and healthy, unconsciously you learned much about how properly to date and marry. Hopefully your parents didn't say, "Do as I say, not as I do," but rather, "Do as I say and as I do." Parents have the power to exert a positive influence on the marriage of their children by the example of their own marriage.

One of the areas where your parents ought to have given you instruction in preparation for dating and marriage is the area of sex, especially because of the day and age in which you are now living. There are many passages in the book of Proverbs where a father gives this instruction to his child. Yet many young adults have never received this instruction, either because their parents were afraid to address this intimate subject with them or because the parents supposed that their children would just figure it out on their own or learn the basics from other kids at school. As an aside, be committed in your own parenting to give this instruction to your children.[1]

Your parents have a further responsibility now that you are of dating age. They are there to help you determine if you are mature enough to date. If not, they may tell you that you cannot date yet. Or they may tell you that you cannot be alone with the one you are interested in, but may only remain close friends and see one another in groups.

---

1   For a helpful book addressing this subject, see Josh & Dottie McDowell, *Straight Talk with Your Kids about Sex* (Eugene, OR: Harvest House Publishers, 2012).

Your parents also have a say in the way in which you date. They set the curfew when you have to be home from a date. They will ask what kinds of things you do on a date and what places you visit. They are there to remind you of your calling to sexual purity in dating.

Of vital concern to your parents is the person whom you date. They can help point you to those they think suitable (although this usually makes young people uninterested). They especially want to guard you from dating someone who is unsuitable. Your father might step in if you, his sixteen-year-old daughter, are asked out by a twenty-five-year-old man. Or he might tell you to put an end to your relationship with an unbelieving girl. Or he might encourage you to reconsider dating someone who is not mature or is a bad influence on you.

Every parent has to balance trust and oversight in the area of dating. There is a danger for parents that they be uninterested in their children's dating and fail to exercise oversight and give direction in this important matter. On the other hand, it is possible for parents to be too distrusting so that they are constantly hovering over their children. When the children are young and first starting to date, they need the close oversight and direction. But as they grow older, as they mature, and as they show themselves trustworthy, there is a gradual relaxing of the oversight. This requires a great deal of wisdom on the part of parents.

THE PLACE OF OTHERS

In addition to the oversight of parents, there are others who have a vested interest in our dating. Certainly our good friends will be interested in whom we are dating. Often we will tell things to our friends that we don't feel comfortable talking about with our parents. We need good friends who will encourage us to date in a holy way and will also help guard us against dating anyone we shouldn't. The wrong kind of friends are those who are encouraging us to do sinful things in our dating or encouraging us to date the wrong people. If they show that their judgment is that impaired, they probably shouldn't be our friends.

The church also is deeply interested in the dating of the young people. The church wants to see strong marriages established in her midst, so she is going to be interested in who the youth are dating. The elders especially have the calling from God to oversee this part of the life of the young people and to see to it that they date and marry in the Lord. Sometimes the youth can be defensive when the elders ask about their dating, but this is not off-limits. The elders are simply exercising good oversight when they probe into this area of life.

All this goes to show that dating is no private matter. You might be tempted to think that the only ones who have a say are yourself and the one you are dating, but this is not true. As members of a body of believers and a covenantal community, your dating lives are open to the loving encouragement and correction of others. This requires you to be humble. "Likewise, ye younger, submit yourselves unto the elder. Yea, all of you be subject one to another, and be clothed with humility: for God resisteth the proud, and giveth grace to the humble" (1 Pet. 5:5).

THE ATTITUDE OF THE YOUTH

So far we've looked at things from the point of view of parents and the church. Now I want to turn to the calling that the young people have toward parents and others who have a concern about their dating. There are three things I want to mention.

1. The wise young person seeks opportunity to date in the sight of others.

The foolish young person of the world dates in secret. He dates a girl without anyone else knowing about it, or he dates her by always being gone with just her. He foolishly avoids the oversight of family and friends (to say nothing of the church). His dating becomes a private, hidden part of his life.

Not so with a wise, mature, Christian young person. Although there are times when he is alone with his girlfriend, this does not characterize their dating as a whole. He is careful to spend time with his and her families, with friends, and with members of the church.

This has the advantage of opening ourselves up to the oversight of others. The people who know us best and love us most can evaluate the person we are potentially going to marry. They can see the way that the two of us interact.

This also has the advantage of truly getting to know the person we are dating. You might learn certain things about a person when you are one-on-one, but nothing tells you who someone really is like that person being around their family. They are most comfortable around parents and siblings. Their guard is down, and they let go of all pretense. Besides, most families seem happy to tell stories about their loved one, especially embarrassing stories.

It's also good to get to know the family of the person we are dating. Our parents and siblings have a huge impact on how we act and think, so it's important to get to know them. A young man might study his future mother-in-law to learn how his future wife might act. A young woman might study her future father-in-law to see what her future husband might be like. Also, if we end up getting married, we are going to be a part of that family. It's important that they know us and we know them.

2. The wise young person seeks out the advice of others.

Not only does the wise young person place himself in situations where he and his date are around others in dating, but he also actively seeks out the advice of others.

The foolish young person of the world does not care about the opinion of others. He doesn't care what his parents think about his girlfriend. He doesn't care what his girlfriend's parents think about him. He doesn't care what his friends say or what her friends say. The only thing that matters is what he thinks.

But the wise young person has a different attitude. Because he is deeply concerned about his future marriage, he welcomes any advice that someone else can give him. He doesn't wait for his parents to voice their opinion of his girlfriend, but he comes to them and says, "Dad and Mom, you've seen my girlfriend a few times now. What do you think? Do you like her? Do you think we are good together? Do you think she will be a good wife someday?" He asks the same thing of his friends: "You guys have known me since grade school. What do you think?" He might even have the courage to ask a pastor or an elder or another member of the church what he thinks. At the very least he might ask for general advice on dating and marriage from someone whom he looks up to in the church.

3. The wise young person heeds the advice of others.

Not only does the wise young person seek the advice of others, he is willing also to follow through on that advice.

The immature young person of the world not only does not want to hear the advice of his parents, but he will not obey it either. If his parents say that he should break up with his girlfriend, he refuses. Or he agrees to do so but continues to date her on the sly.

The wise young person values the advice of older, wiser people in his life, not only in dating but in every area of life. Countless times the book of Proverbs extols the wisdom of the child of God who is teachable and heeds the advice and correction of parents and friends (for example, Prov. 1:5; 9:9). There may be times when he does not follow through on that advice if he is convinced that it is not right. But that advice weighs heavy upon him, and he gives serious thought to heeding it.

The wise young person also has a deep appreciation for his place in the church of Christ. He recognizes that God has placed him in the fellowship of the body so that other members can care for him (see 1 Cor. 12:25). He delights in assembling with other believers who "provoke [him] unto love and to good works" (Heb. 10:24). He is grateful for the elders who advise him about his dating during family visitation, because he knows that "they watch for [his soul], as they that must give account" (13:17).

In all this, the wise young person realizes that he is not always the best judge of himself or of circumstances in his life. We are often blind to our own faults, as the psalmist confesses: "Who can understand his errors? cleanse thou me from secret faults" (Ps. 19:12). We are often blind in the matter of dating and love. We need a fresh pair of eyes on the situation. We need someone who knows us, loves us, and can give objective advice that is truly in our best interests.

It's a sad fact that many young people refuse to listen to the counsel of their parents and friends and officebearers. I've seen it many times. A young man starts dating a young woman and they "fall in love," but very quickly the people around them see that this is not a healthy relationship. His parents tell him, "You shouldn't be with her." His friends say, "You guys don't seem right for each other." The elders step in and say, "We advise you to break up." But stubbornly the two persist. They say that no else understands. They get married. But when the "love" cools, the marriage ends in divorce. Only then does he say with deep regret, "If only I had listened to my parents so many years ago!"

Our parents are not always right, but they usually possess a good deal of wisdom and common sense acquired through years of experience. We do well to involve them in the process of dating and to value their advice. What a blessing on the wedding day when both families can say, "We've vetted these young people, and we are glad that they are marrying one another! We are glad to welcome them into our family!"

DISCUSSION QUESTIONS

1. What is the place of your parents in dating?

2. What benefits are there in having others involved in the dating process? What dangers are there in rejecting the involvement of others?

3. Getting advice about dating from a parent can feel awkward at times. In what ways can you help your parents in this so that it is not so difficult? In what ways can your parents help you so that it is not so difficult?

4. Talk to your parents or a wise older couple from church about their dating life. What advice would they give you?

CHAPTER 7

WHAT ABOUT SEX?

'm guessing that many of you have been anticipating this
chapter. Those who are dating have probably wondered at
some time, "Where are the boundaries? What can we do with
each other? What can we not do? How far is too far?"

This is certainly a major concern of your parents (if not,
it should be!). They have probably wondered, "What is my
son doing on his dates? How is my daughter being treated by
her boyfriend? Have they maintained the sexual boundaries
that are in place?"

Sex is a major concern in dating. It is not the only concern, but it certainly ranks high on the list.

Some have decided against dating largely for this reason
and rather choose courtship. They feel that their young adults
are not able to handle the sexual pressures, so they remove

any opportunity for this to happen by never allowing courting couples to be alone.

But what does this pressure mean for those who think
dating is legitimate? Do we resign ourselves to the fact that
the crossing of sexual boundaries is going to happen, even
though we wish it wouldn't? Do we have no boundaries in
place, no way of helping defend against these powerful
temptations?

I certainly hope not. My point in this chapter is to expose
and condemn the sexual sins that the world tolerates and
even encourages in its dating, but also to spell out some of
the ways in which you can date as a Christian in a way that
promotes purity and self-control.

THE DANGERS

Christian young people face tremendous pressures from the
world around them to engage in sex before marriage. Their
classmates at college, their fellow employees at the office, and
their coworkers on the job site speak openly of the sexual
sin in which they engage. They curiously enquire about the
amount of sex the Christian young person has. They laugh
uproariously when they hear that the Christian does not
engage in fornication but is saving himself or herself for marriage. This can make the child of God feel small and stupid,
and the resolve to preserve purity might crumble.

Apart from any pressure from the world, the child of God
has all he can handle with his own sinful nature. Especially

in the mid-teens, the human body is a rage of hormones. The sexual urges are powerful, especially in those who have not yet fully learned the ability to control themselves. Even as they get older, those sexual desires remain strong.

When you put a young man and a young woman together in dating, you have a situation where both have an intense physical, sexual attraction to each other. The following activities may be present:

- Kissing and close physical contact on the first date.
- Sexting, that is, sending sexually explicit messages.
- Close, intimate hugging.
- Intense, passionate kissing, often for long periods of time ("making out").
- "Petting," or touching one another's bodies, including privates, to excite sexual desires.
- Oral sex.
- Sex.

If a couple begins to engage in some of these activities, they find it more difficult to resist going further. That's the case because our sex drive works on a "positive-feedback" system. What that means is that each time you are stimulated, it doesn't satisfy but only makes you want more and more.[1]

---

1   Phillips, *Holding Hands*, 149–50.

Too often the question that's asked is, "How far can we go? How far is too far?" But even asking that question reveals a weakness in one's soul. It's the wrong question to ask.

When a young man and woman begin to push these sexual boundaries, they will often come up with excuses for why this behavior is permissible. They might whisper in each other's ear, "I love you," as if their love for each other allows them to do what they are doing. They might think, "This is how I show him I love him," or, "This is how I need to be shown love." They might think, "This will strengthen our relationship and bring us closer together." They might be afraid: "If I don't do this, I'm going to lose him. He's going to look for someone else, and then I'll be alone." They might argue, "This is an important way of knowing whether we are compatible and should get married."

In spite of these excuses, when two people engage in this behavior, there are consequences. The great lie of the devil is that he makes sin look attractive and fun and he wants us to believe that we can participate without consequences. But there are consequences. Obviously there are the potential consequences of having a child out of wedlock or of contracting a sexually transmitted disease. The world is concerned about these things, but these are not the consequences I have most in mind.

Engaging in sex before marriage always leaves one with a wounded and scarred conscience. After engaging in sex with a boyfriend or girlfriend, there is the potential to break up later, with either or both of you marrying someone else. You enter into the marriage with baggage, which often presents serious problems. For example, a husband whose wife engaged in sex with a previous boyfriend may wonder if she thinks about the other man when they are together. Or a wife whose husband engaged in sex with a previous girlfriend may wonder how she measures up to the other woman.

SHE WORE WHITE

Traditionally a bride wears a white dress on her wedding day. The white dress symbolizes her purity (and, by implication, the purity of the groom). I want you to wear white at your wedding, and to do so confident that it is an accurate symbol of your clean conscience and sexual purity as a couple before God.

That means you must avoid all sexual sin in your dating. The word of God is clear that any sexual activity before or outside of the bond of marriage is sin. First Corinthians 6:18 commands, "Flee fornication." Ephesians 5:3 says, "But fornication, and all uncleanness, or covetousness, let it not be once named among you, as becometh saints." The point here is that there ought not to be even a hint of fornication or sexual uncleanness in our lives, since these things are not compatible with our being saints (holy ones).

Jesus shows that fornication is more than just the physical act when he says, "Ye have heard that it was said by them of old time, Thou shalt not commit adultery: but I say unto you, That whosoever looketh on a woman to lust after her hath committed adultery with her already in his heart" (Matt. 5:27–28).

The Heidelberg Catechism is helpful in its explanation of the seventh commandment in Lord's Day 41: "Doth God forbid in this commandment only adultery and such like gross sins? Since both our body and soul are temples of the Holy Ghost, He commands us to preserve them pure and holy; therefore He forbids all unchaste actions, gestures, words, thoughts, desires, and whatever can entice men thereto."[2]

Positively, the word of God makes plain that all our sexual energy is to be directed toward our spouse within the bounds of marriage. Proverbs 5 says, "Drink waters out of thine own cistern, and running waters out of thine own well…Let thy fountain be blessed: and rejoice with the wife of thy youth. Let her be as the loving hind and pleasant roe; let her breasts satisfy thee at all times; and be thou ravished always with her love" (vv. 15, 18–19). Hebrews 13:4 says, "Marriage is honourable in all, and the bed undefiled."

In our dating we must be careful not to steal or give away this good gift that God has intended for our marriage. I believe the following six ideas will help.

1. Treat one another as brother and sister.

When you date a person for a length of time, you begin to feel that you have an exclusive right to that person. You feel committed to one another and would be justly angry if the other

---

2   Heidelberg Catechism Q&A 109, in *Confessions and Church Order*, 131.

started flirting with someone else. This sense of commitment increases the longer you are dating and especially when you are engaged.

But this does not extend to the body of that other person. No matter how long you have been dating, no matter if you are engaged, no matter if it's the day before your wedding, the body of the other person does not belong to you. His or her body only becomes yours when you are married. It's happened that two people who seemed destined to marry, two people who have even been engaged, don't get married in the end. Any number of things can come up to bring an end to a relationship. It is never "safe" to assume that the body of the other person will eventually become yours so that you can begin to take advantage of it prematurely. To do so would be to "defraud" the other person's future spouse of what belongs only to him or her (1 Thess. 4:6).

Until you get married, it is best to deal with one another physically as a brother with a sister. The fact of the matter is that you are brother and sister in the Lord. Only do things with one another if you would do the same things with your blood brother or sister. The apostle Paul tells Timothy to treat "the elder women as mothers; the younger as sisters, with all purity" (1 Tim. 5:2).

What does that mean practically? It means that you can hold hands and give one another a hug. It means that you can kiss, albeit in a much more restrained manner than most dating couples do. Gone are the intense, passionate, my-tongue-in-your-mouth kisses. Gone are the "make-out sessions" that go on for half an hour. You wouldn't do that with your sibling, so don't do it with your boyfriend or girlfriend. It means that you can speak kindly and compassionately to one another, expressing even your love for one another, but not using your words to stir up sexual desires. It means that you keep your hands off of any sensitive areas of the other's body and do not engage in any "petting." It means absolutely no oral sex. Apparently there are some Christian young people who have a question about whether or not oral sex really counts as sex.[3] There shouldn't be any question: oral sex is sex and therefore is off limits in dating. It means that there is absolutely no sex.

Keep this idea in mind—treat one another as brother and sister—and it will keep you from sexual sin in your dating.

2. Focus on the relationship.

This point is nicely summarized in the following quotation: "Before you touch her body, touch her heart and mind."[4]

What this means is that the focus of your thoughts and attention in dating ought to be on your relationship, getting to know one another better, and building a strong friendship. The focus ought not to be on the physical and sexual.

Think about dating and marriage like a cake. When you

---

3   McDowell, *Straight Talk*, 165–68.
4   C. J. Mahaney, quoted in Douglas Sean O'Donnell, *The Song of Solomon: An Invitation to Intimacy* (Wheaton, IL: Crossway, 2012), 37.

want to make a cake, the first thing you focus on is making the cake itself. Only when the cake is out of the oven and has had time to cool do you put the icing on the top. Icing tastes good on its own, but it was never meant to stand on its own as an independent meal. It was meant to serve as the topping on a finished cake.

The same is true regarding sex, dating, and marriage. The friendship between a man and woman is like the cake itself. Sex is the icing. It is not meant to be enjoyed on its own but is intended by God only for the delight of husband and wife in marriage and as an expression of their love and friendship. Even in marriage, when there is a breakdown in the relationship, that is expressed in the sexual life of husband and wife. If husband and wife are fighting and being selfish, they are not going to jump into bed together. But if there is harmony between husband and wife—their friendship is strong, and they are willing to give of themselves for one another—that will be expressed in a strong, healthy sex life. Sex apart from that marriage relationship of friendship and love is carnal, animalistic, and sinful.

That's why in your dating you ought to be focusing solely on building the relationship between the two of you. Bake the cake first, and let the icing wait. You will have plenty of time once you are married to enjoy the delights of sex. But let that wait until the proper time when you are one in marriage. Until then, focus on getting to know one another, working through your differences, and growing together spiritually.

3. Set clear boundaries.

When you begin to date someone seriously, you ought to lay down some boundaries and set some ground rules. This means that after a few dates, you should have an open conversation with each other about boundaries. You have to be frank and yet careful. The purpose here is not to stir up sexual thoughts, but to help guard each other from falling into temptation.

Start the conversation this way: "I really like you and am excited to keep seeing you. I appreciate how you respect me, and I hope you know that I respect you. For that reason, I don't want us to do anything that would be disrespectful and sinful. Can we talk about some boundaries?" Then talk together about where the limits are. Talk about what is acceptable and what is going too far. Having this conversation, and agreeing on what is acceptable and what is unacceptable, will go a long way in helping guard your hearts and bodies. This might seem intimidating, but remember that as a Christian, you date differently.

Sometimes your parents might see the wisdom in having this conversation with you and the one you are dating. Perhaps your father will go out for coffee with the young man who is interested in you and explain to him how he ought to be treating you.[5] Or dad and mom might sit down with you and your girlfriend and explain what is expected of you from

---

5   One book that promotes this idea is Dennis Rainey, *Interviewing Your Daughter's Date: 8 Steps to No Regrets* (Little Rock, AR: Family Life Publishing, 2007).

the word of God. As young people you have to be open to this exercise of your parents' authority and be grateful for it, uncomfortable as it might be in the moment.

Remember that, in the end, sexual purity is not about rule keeping. Those boundaries will certainly be a help, but ultimately it is a matter of the heart (Mark 7:20–23). Guard your heart with all diligence (Prov. 4:23)!

4. Maintain accountability.

It's important in all of our life to seek out others to keep us accountable, and the area of dating is no different. We need others to help hold us accountable to the standards of purity and self-control.

This accountability begins with your boyfriend or girl-friend. If you have talked openly about the boundaries in your dating, then you can help hold one another to that standard. If one of you is weak and wants to push the limits, the other one can gently remind him or her of what you agreed upon: "As much as I want to be with you someday, we agreed that we weren't going to do that until we are married."

Those who are living under their parents' roof also have that added level of accountability. Parental authority is not something to chafe under but something to welcome. The presence of parents can be a powerful deterrent to sexual temptation. This, again, is reason to spend time with one another's families. Not only do you get to know one another better that way, but you are in an environment where sexual sin is far from your mind.

One of the practical ways that we can maintain accountability is by never dating in the dark, that is, by never being alone in a room while the lights are off. This is something that my parents emphasized with me when I was dating. Nothing good ever happens when the lights are off. Purity and holiness are things that belong to the light and are rarely found in the cover of night. Be committed to dating with the lights on, always.

5. The man must lead.

In the matter of sex in dating, as well as every other aspect of the relationship, the man must show himself to be a leader. Part of being a leader means protecting those who are under your care. If while you were on a date a deranged killer or a serial rapist attacked your girlfriend, you would fight tooth and nail to protect her. But not only do you have the calling to protect her physically, you also have the calling to protect her spiritually. If you truly care about her, you will not ask her to do anything sinful but will strive with all your might to preserve her in purity. If you love her, you will sacrifice any sexual urges you might have for her spiritual wellbeing.

The man who urges, coerces, manipulates, and pressures his girlfriend into sexual sin shows himself to be weak and not a leader. In spite of his insistence that he loves her and wants to show her his love, he does not truly love her with a self-sacrificing, Christ-like love. He has a lot of lust, but little love. Ladies, if you have such a boyfriend, confront him openly and call him to repentance. If he does not change, dump him. He's not good husband material. Find another man who will treat you with respect and be a strong, spiritual leader.

6. Thank God for his goodness.

In forbidding sexual activity by those who are unmarried, God is not being stifling or cruel. Yet that's the way the world portrays God's commands, and that's often the way we are tempted to think. We might wonder, "Why would God give me these strong sexual desires and then withhold this intense pleasure from me while I'm single? How is that good?"

The truth is that God is not being cruel but rather is being good to us. This is true of all God's commandments. Not only are they what he demands of us, but they are also the way that is truly good for us. God's forbidding of sexual activity before marriage is good because it serves the protection of our consciences, the protection of our marriages, and the protection of our children.

So rather than viewing chastity as a chore, receive it with thanksgiving from God.

GRACE FOR THE GUILTY

Perhaps there are some reading this who are thinking, "I wish I had read this earlier in my life. I wish I would have listened to my parents' advice and the word of God. But I was weak and gave in and fell into sexual temptation. I pushed the boundaries with my girlfriend. I did things with my boyfriend that I'm terribly ashamed of."

The word of God has something to say to these young people. The word of God to those who are truly sorry for these sins and repent of them is that there is forgiveness with God. Our guilty stains are washed away in the precious blood of Christ. Even the sins that leave the deepest scars and greatest shame are forgiven and buried in the depths of the sea.

Not only does God forgive us for Christ's sake, but he also sanctifies and cleanses us by his Holy Spirit. He delivers us from the power of sin, so that we are no longer slaves to it. He breaks the power of sexual sins and gives the grace of self-control. It is important to remember that as powerful as sexual temptation is, the power of Christ at work within us is far greater.

One of the powerful passages that teaches this is 1 Corinthians 6:9–11: "Know ye not that the unrighteous shall not inherit the kingdom of God? Be not deceived: neither fornicators, nor idolaters, nor adulterers, nor effeminate, nor abusers of themselves with mankind…shall inherit the kingdom of God. And such were some of you: but ye are washed, but ye are sanctified, but ye are justified in the name of the Lord Jesus, and by the Spirit of our God." Paul says of the Corinthian Christians, "But such were some of you!" Some were guilty of adultery and even of homosexual sin. But now they are justified and sanctified.

If you are a child of God who has fallen into these sins, do not despair. In his grace God forgives. By his grace he sanctifies. In gratitude for such a salvation, flee from sexual sin, live pure and holy, and stand on your wedding day in the white robes of Christ's righteousness.

DISCUSSION QUESTIONS

1. Find three more Bible passages that speak directly to the topic of sexual purity. What do you learn from them?

2. What are some excuses that we might be using to justify pushing the sexual boundaries?

3. What are some things that Christian couples commonly do in dating that ought not to be?

4. What are some of the consequences that God sends when we engage in sex before marriage?

5. What are five ideas that can help us keep this good gift for marriage?

6. What does it mean that sex is the icing on the cake of the relationship?

7. What should you do if you have fallen into sexual sin?

CHAPTER 8

WHAT IF I'M SINGLE ALL MY LIFE?

t's worth taking the time to talk about the single life in a book on dating. For one thing, all who are presently dating are still single, and some of the things that we talk about in this chapter apply to them. But it's also worthwhile because there are some Christians who date and never marry and some who never date at all. How are they to live as singles?

A word of instruction and encouragement is needed because of how difficult the single life can be. Part of the difficulty is due to the world in which we live. The world's view of single life is 180 degrees in the opposite direction of what God says in his word. The world preaches that single life is a life of freedom, without the bondage of marriage and children. A single person is free to do whatever he pleases, as long as it is "safe." To their shame, many Reformed churches have adopted the thinking of the world. They say that single young people have a God-given sexual nature and it is wrong to deny them the use of it. So long as they are in a committed relationship with someone else and plan to get married in the future, they are free to live together and exercise their God-given sexual natures. This is a threat to Reformed singles, and it is necessary for us to address them from the word of God.

The single life also can be difficult because of a weakness that can be found in the church. The weakness is that we talk about married life and childrearing so much that we virtually ignore the other members of the church who are not married. The result is that the singles often feel neglected and feel like misfits. They feel like they really don't have a place in the church, or at least not a very important place.

First Corinthians 7 is the outstanding passage of God's word that addresses single life. As is clear from verse 1, Paul is answering specific questions regarding marriage that the church in Corinth asked him. This was an important issue for that church because they were living in the midst of a godless, debauched city. Fornication was so common in the city that it was viewed as something like eating and drinking. Even in other parts of the world the sin of fornication was known as "corinthianizing." The apostle Paul answers their questions by giving very down-to-earth, practical instruction. He is bold to speak the truth of God's word regarding sex, marriage, and single life.

This is what we need today. We live in the midst of a world that is equally godless and debauched. Some may be squeamish about the subject of sex and not want such bluntness, but failing to do so in this world is inexcusable. We need the down-to-earth, practical wisdom of the word to guide us not only in marriage, but also in single life.

THE REALITY OF THE SINGLE LIFE

In 1 Corinthians 7, Paul is addressing a special class of singles. There are some who willingly choose for themselves the single life. They have decided that they will live the rest of their lives as a single. This was true of the apostle Paul. He was never married but chose to live his entire life as a single.

Those who do so must meet the essential qualification: they must have the gift of self-control. First Corinthians 7:7 says, "For I would that all men were even as I myself. But every man hath his proper gift of God, one after this manner, and another after that." In verse 9 he speaks of that proper gift as the ability to "contain." Some members of the church have received from God the special gift of sexual self-control so that they do not have a strong sexual desire or sex drive. Those with this gift may choose to live their life as a single. But the person who willingly chooses the single life must have that essential qualification.

However, the vast majority of singles in the church do

have a strong sexual drive and they do desire to marry. They pray to God regularly to bring them a spouse. But although they have this desire, God has not yet led them to a spouse, and they continue to live as a single.

This is a very difficult trial. It is difficult to see friends and family getting older, marrying, and having children. It is difficult to face struggles alone, without a spouse to walk through this life with them.

These singles are called by God to look for one to marry. Verse 9 says, "But if they cannot contain, let them marry: for it is better to marry than to burn." Ordinarily, it is not good for a man to be without a wife (Gen. 2:18). This does not mean that a single man or woman who desires to be married ought to marry whomever. They may not be in such a rush to get married that they marry badly. It is better for them to remain single than to enter into a bad marriage. Nevertheless, if they don't have this gift, they must look to get married.

For some singles, there are wrong ways of thinking that must be addressed. First, it is possible that they are not married because they are too choosy. They've set unrealistic standards in their search for a spouse so that no one meets their lofty standards. Several years ago I listened as a young man I'll call "Alex" talked at length about his desire for a wife. In the course of the conversation, Alex began to list all the qualifications his future wife had to possess. At the time I thought he was joking and found it humorous. But looking back, I realize he was serious, and I find that attitude troubling.

Another danger for singles is that they do not really make an effort to get out and try to get to know others, to ask someone on a date, or to look beyond the small circle of people they already know.

It is also possible that a single person looks at the hardships of marriage and rearing children and therefore does not look for a spouse. He does not have the gift for singleness, but neither is he looking for a spouse.

If you have the gift of self-control, remain single. But if you do not have this gift, look for a spouse and wait upon the Lord to see whether or not he will bring you one.

THE GOODNESS OF THE SINGLE LIFE

No matter what the reason is for singleness—whether you have the gift of self-control, or you desire a spouse but have not received one—God says that the single life is good and honorable.

This is something that the church has not always properly emphasized. This is due to our emphasis upon the importance of marriage, the family, and children. This is a right emphasis. But it is possible for us so to overemphasize marriage and the family that we do harm to the single members. Often our attitude makes the singles feel as if they are second-class citizens of the kingdom of heaven. They are often neglected in the life of the church so that they feel like misfits. Often this can be the attitude of parents as well. They become horrified when their child passes through his twenties without being married and sometimes without even having a date. They put pressure upon their child to marry. What can happen is that the single person so wants to avoid the single life that he rushes into a disastrous marriage because he thinks anything is better than being alone.

But God says in 1 Corinthians 7 that the single life is good. Verses 7–8 say, "For I would that all men were even as I myself [that is, unmarried]...I say therefore to the unmarried and widows, It is good for them if they abide even as I." The single life is good in the eyes of God.

If it is good in the eyes of God, then it must be viewed as something good in the eyes of the church. The church must continue to preach the importance of marriage and the family. It is in this way that God ordinarily gathers his church, as he gathers his elect in the line of continued generations. But the church must also be careful to receive and accept the singles. Marriage is not an absolute requirement and is not the only option for a child of God. We must include the singles in the regular life of the church.

There is also application here for the single members of the church. Be encouraged that you are not second-class citizens of the kingdom, less important than those who are married and have children. God has seen fit to make you a single, and he says that that is good and honorable. This is how you must look at the single life as well. Remember that in heaven there will be no more marriage, which shows that marriage is not everything. What will remain in heaven is our marriage to Christ. This is the most important thing for both singles and those who are married: you are united to Christ now and forever. Rejoice in this spiritual union!

THE CALLING OF THE SINGLE LIFE

Those who are single have certain responsibilities before God. Consider the following three things.

1. Their calling, first of all, is to serve Christ and his church.

This is what 1 Corinthians 7 says makes the single life good. Verses 32–33 say, "But I would have you without carefulness. He that is unmarried careth for the things that belong to the Lord, how he may please the Lord: but he that is married careth for the things that are of the world, how he may please his wife." Verse 34 says, "There is difference also between a wife and a virgin. The unmarried woman careth for the things of the Lord, that she may be holy both in body and in spirit: but she that is married careth for the things of the world, how she may please her husband."

The difference here is not absolute, but a matter of degree. Those who are married care for the things of the world. This is not saying that marriage is inherently sinful and worldly-minded but is simply acknowledging that those who are married have many earthly concerns, chiefly how they may please their spouse and children. Much of their time is spent with such necessary things as a job, money, house, clothes, doctor bills, Christian school tuition, and time for the family. The one who is married must also dedicate his time and energy to the service of Christ and the church, but he does so while also exhausting himself in the service of his family.

This is different for the one who is single. The one who is single does not have the same amount of earthly cares that the married do. They do not have a spouse to care for and children to provide for. This does not mean that the singles can be carefree and live an irresponsible life, doing whatever they please. With the extra time and energy and money that they have, they are called to serve the church. They have the ability to serve the church with less distraction, and for this reason the single life is good.

This is important for the singles to remember. The fact that you are a single is not an excuse for you to withdraw from the life of the church. God has placed you into this unique position in the church, and he calls you to be an active member of the church. You are called to use your abilities and time and even money for the good of the church. You are not unimportant members of the church but have an important place and are useful to the kingdom. Singleness is not for enhanced selfishness, but for enhanced service.

I've read about a single woman who outfitted her house with a guest room and rec room for family and friends in need of a place to stay and filled her home with games, toys, and even a high chair so that any guest would be comfortable. She was committed to serving as a single.[1]

2. Singles have the calling to honor the institution of marriage by living chaste and pure.

God forbids singles from engaging in any sexual activity before or outside of marriage. God wants all of his children either to enter into marriage as virgins or to live their whole lives as virgins.

The chaste single will not only preserve his virginity, he will also avoid anything that may lead to sexual sin. This includes such things as worldly dancing, listening to music that uses sexual lyrics to arouse desire, watching dramas and movies on TV or Netflix that contain sexual scenes, dressing immodestly, and viewing pornography. The forbidding of fornication also means no sexual gratification of self (masturbation).

You who are single must flee from fornication. Do not in pride think that you can stand up to these temptations without falling. Allowing yourself to remain in these situations only feeds your old man of sin and makes him stronger. The way of conquering these temptations is most often by cowardice. You turn and you run from anything that is remotely connected to sexual sin. Flee fornication!

---

1 Robert D. Wolgemuth, *Lies Men Believe: And the Truth That Sets Them Free* (Chicago: Moody Publishers, 2018), 142.

The reason God requires of singles that they live sexually pure is because they are the temple of the Holy Spirit (1 Cor. 6:19). Jesus Christ has poured out his Holy Spirit into our hearts, so that our bodies and souls are temples of the Holy Spirit. Christ lives within us. When we commit the sin of fornication, we are joining our body and soul to a harlot or adulterer. This means that when we fornicate, we are, in a sense, attempting to join Jesus Christ to that harlot or adulterer. This is the grossest dishonor of Jesus Christ! For that reason, live pure and holy in single life.

The other reason for this command is that God has given marriage as the picture of his relationship with his church. Sexual intimacy is reserved only for marriage between husband and wife because it is a picture of the spiritual intimacy that God enjoys with his bride. When we engage in sexual sin, whether as a married person or a single, we are destroying the picture of Christ and his church. For this reason, God requires those who are single to flee fornication. Show your love for God's institution of marriage by keeping yourself as a virgin until you are married.

3. Singles have the calling to learn contentment with God's will for them.

There's no doubt that the single life is hard. Some singles are severely tempted to respond to this trial in discontentment. They become bitter and angry at being cheated by God out of marriage. They despair at having their hopes and dreams dashed. They may be tempted to think that if they would just find a spouse, they would be happy.

But that's not true. One pastor writes, "If you cannot be contented in singleness, you will not be contented in marriage."[2] Singleness does not force us to be bitter. Like every other trial, it simply squeezes out what is already in our hearts. If we are discontented as a single, marriage is not going to fix that. The fact is that marriage and parenthood can also be trials. They are a great blessing, but they come with their own set of unique challenges and struggles. Singles must not think that if they could only get married, their life would be better. No person, however precious, can supply what is found in God alone.

So, just like every Christian, singles must learn to be content in their unique circumstances. What the apostle Paul says in Philippians 4:11 applies to singles: "Not that I speak in respect of want: for I have learned, in whatsoever state I am, therewith to be content." Contentment has been defined as "that sweet, inward, quiet, gracious frame of spirit, which freely submits to and delights in God's wise and fatherly disposal in every condition."[3] It is peace found not in our circumstances but in our sovereign, wise, loving Father.

This is a lesson that the single must constantly be learning. Through prayer (2 Cor. 12:8–10) and constantly bringing his thoughts to rest on God (Isa. 26:3), he can and does learn contentment in the single life.

---

2   Phillips, *Holding Hands*, 170.
3   Jeremiah Burroughs, quoted in Phillips, *Holding Hands*, 169.

THE POSSIBILITY OF THE SINGLE LIFE

This is a hard, difficult, narrow way that God requires of singles. They confess that they don't have the gift of self-control. A man desires a wife but no woman ever says yes. A woman desires a husband but no man ever proposes to her. This is a tremendous difficulty for them.

So we wonder, "How is this possible?" The answer is that living the good, pure single life is possible by the grace of God. There is in Christ the grace and strength so that you can live the single life. Paul follows the words we just quoted from Philippians 4 with these familiar words: "I can do all things through Christ which strengtheneth me" (v. 13). Trust that God's grace will be sufficient for sexual self-control. Learn to view the single life not simply as a cross to bear but as the specific way of life in which you are to glorify God. Seize singleness as the opportunity to serve the Lord Jesus more fully than would be possible if you were married.[4]

---

4   These last lines are adapted from David J. Engelsma, *Better to Marry: Sex and Marriage in I Corinthians 6 & 7*, 2nd ed. (Jenison, MI: Reformed Free Publishing Association, 2014), 44.

DISCUSSION QUESTIONS

1. What are some dangers singles can fall into that keep them from dating?

2. In what ways can singles serve the church?

3. In what ways can the church further include single members?

4. Are there any older singles in your church right now? What more can you and your friends be doing to interact with them and serve them well as brothers and sisters in Christ?

CHAPTER 9

WHEN DO I GET MARRIED?

I am not a naturally decisive person. I hem and haw over the smallest decisions, going back and forth, weighing the pros and cons. But there were especially three decisions in my life that gave me the most angst. One was deciding which college to go to after high school. The second was determining how to answer the calls I received after I graduated from seminary. And the third was when exactly to propose to my wife.

Don't get me wrong. I knew I wanted to marry her. There was no doubt in my mind that she was way out of my league (further years of marriage have only confirmed this). But I was not sure when was the best time to get married. We had been dating for over three years. But I was a student who had only finished two years of college, and I was facing two more years of undergraduate study and four years of seminary.

Besides, I was on the college basketball team, and I knew that if I got married, it would not work to continue to devote so much time to the game.

After much prayer and evaluating of priorities, I finally proposed, and I have no regrets about that decision. But it was a very difficult and uncertain time.

I'm sure not everyone has as difficult a time with proposing as I did. But I'm guessing that there are some out there who have some of the same questions and concerns. This concluding chapter is intended to give some guidance for navigating the end of dating and the beginning of marriage.

GROWING

Before we get to the part about proposing, let's first look briefly at how a healthy relationship would ordinarily grow and develop over the course of your dating.[1]

1. The friendship stage

Often a relationship begins with two people becoming friends. Perhaps you go to the same church and are involved in the same activities. Perhaps you go to the same school. Perhaps you spend time with the same group of friends. As you spend time together in your group of friends, you get to know the other person better. You realize you enjoy spending time together. You realize there is a mutual interest in one another.

---

1 Chediak, *With One Voice*, 111–34.

As the friendship develops, it eventually leads to the next step of actually dating.

The amount of time spent in this stage will vary depending on age and maturity. Especially for those who are young (fifteen to seventeen years old, for example), this stage ought to last a lot longer than it will for those who are in their twenties or thirties. As a teenager you are not in a position to marry, so rather than moving a relationship along too fast, spend more time getting to know one another as friends. Spend time together in large groups of friends and keep your emotions from running ahead.

2. The early dating stage

Some will jump right to this stage by asking someone out on a "blind date," when you really don't know each other that well. Others will progress from being friends to starting to date.

If you reach this stage and go on a few dates, there is an understanding of being exclusive. You are not dating anyone else, nor are you looking for anyone else. It also means that you have marriage as the goal. You are beginning to determine if this person is the one you could marry.

At this stage you should not be spending a lot of time together, especially if you are young. The amount of time you spend together ought to be determined by the level of seriousness in the relationship. Since you aren't very serious at this point, don't spend every weekend together. Don't talk or text or connect via social media every day.

Because the relationship is just beginning, there also ought not to be a significant amount of emotional intimacy at this point. Get to know one another, but don't swim too deep too fast.

Let me give a word of caution in this regard about praying together. It might be good to pray briefly together for God's blessing upon your time with each other, but there can be a danger in praying long, deep prayers together already at this early stage. This leaves the impression that you are already a couple. That will come later. If you do pray together, keep it short and focused merely on that specific date.

3. The later dating stage

If you continue to date and both parties are still interested, eventually you transition into the later stages of dating. This is when you start to spend more time together. This is when you start to share more with the other person about your hopes and dreams, your fears and struggles. It is not yet a guarantee of marriage, but you are working more deliberately toward that goal.

This may be a time to tell one another that you love each other. Be careful with doing so. Remember that love is much more than just a warm, fuzzy feeling or an attraction to another person. Love views another person as delightful and precious even when they are unlovable on account of their sins. It is a commitment to sacrifice self for the sake of the other's wellbeing. Know what you mean when you utter those weighty words: "I love you."

4. The engagement stage

After you've dated for a time and gotten to know one another well, eventually you will get engaged. We'll talk about this more in the rest of this chapter. One thing to note: after getting engaged, speak soon to your pastor to set up pre-marriage counseling meetings. The purpose of these meetings is to help you focus your attention on your upcoming marriage, not just the hoopla surrounding the wedding.

SEPARATING

One more topic should be discussed before we get to engagement. That's the painful subject of breaking up.

At some stage in the dating process, you may come to the realization that you ought not to marry the person you are presently dating. Maybe he is not spiritually mature. Maybe she is struggling with habitual sins. Maybe you simply don't enjoy spending time with him. If, after much thought and prayer and even counsel from others, you are convinced that you cannot marry this person, then you must break up.

When you know this, don't beat around the bush. Don't prolong a bad relationship because you are afraid of breaking it off or because of a fear of being alone. Be upfront with the other person and explain clearly the reasons for the breakup.

Also, as much as possible, do this in person and not over the phone or via text message or social media. Be respectful of the other person and do them the courtesy of talking face-to-face.

In addition, once the relationship is over, protect the reputation of the one you dated. It has happened that after a nasty breakup, one person gossips and smears the reputation of the other so that no one ever wants to date him or her again. Do what you can to protect one another's reputation. The sixth commandment forbids that by your words you dishonor, hate, or wound the other, and the ninth commandment requires that you defend and promote his or her honor and good character, even if you are no longer dating.[2]

Finally, if you date well, a breakup will not be filled with unnecessary pain. If you pushed the boundaries sexually or became emotionally intimate prematurely, a breakup will bring on deep regret and shame. Breakups are hard enough as it is; don't make it worse by dating poorly. Remember the importance of dating differently.

PROPOSING

One question a young man is going to face is, "How do I propose?" It seems like there is an increasing amount of pressure placed on him to scheme up some elaborate proposal that is social media worthy. There ought not to be such pressure. If

---

2   See the explanations of these commandments in the Heidelberg Catechism, Q&A 105–107, 112 (*Confessions and Church Order*, 129–31, 133).

you have the time, money, and creativity to dream up a big proposal, go for it. But don't be embarrassed about a simple proposal either.

The one thing to keep in mind is that you shouldn't propose to a young woman unless you have first met with her dad and asked his permission to do so. This shows that you acknowledge her to be under her father's authority and that you respect that authority. If a father is not ready to give permission and give his blessing on the marriage, the young man and woman must submit and seek to work through whatever issues he sees. Rushing into an engagement without the knowledge and blessing of parents does not bode well for the future.

The other important question that a young man is going to face is, "When do I propose?" Obviously everyone's situation is unique, and I cannot give a blanket statement on when is the proper time to get engaged. I would ask that you keep these two things in mind.

First, don't get engaged too soon. Make sure that you are mature and ready for marriage. Make sure that you have taken enough time to get to know one another thoroughly. Ask the difficult questions, and work through any differences. Take things slowly. Circumstances may differ depending on how old you are. If you started dating in high school, you are probably going to need more time to mature. If you are in your late twenties, you may be able to get engaged in less than a year's time. But, generally speaking, don't rush the engagement.

Second, don't wait too long to get engaged. There are many dangers that come into play when delaying an engagement. If you know one another well, and know that you want to get married, then get engaged. If you wait too long, your emotional connection with one another is going to grow stronger and stronger, and you might be tempted into pushing the boundaries sexually. "It is better to marry than to burn [with sexual desires]" (1 Cor. 7:9).

There is a troubling trend in society to delay getting married. The average age of marriage in 1960 was 22.8 for men and 20.3 for women. In 2003 the average age was 28 for men and 26 for women. This may be due to things such as college education and careers, but there is also the factor of "delayed adolescence." This means that there are lower expectations on twenty-year-olds and an extended period of irresponsibility.[3]

Reformed pastor Kevin DeYoung has some helpful things to say about this matter.[4] He warns that if you wait too long to get engaged, you extend childhood and childish behavior. There is nothing like getting married and having children to make a young man and young woman grow up into maturity. But if this is pushed back, it only prolongs immature, selfish living.

---

3   Chediak, *With One Voice*, 13–25. For a secular perspective, see Lev Grossman, "Grow Up? Not So Fast," *Time* (January 16, 2005), http://content.time.com/time/printout/0,8816,1018089,00.html.

4   DeYoung, *Just Do Something*, 110–112.

Another warning he gives is that when you delay an engagement, it negatively affects women with respect to their future careers. If a young woman knows that she is going to be married soon and potentially be a mother, she may choose not to go to college and rack up large student loans. But if an engagement is pushed off, she is left in a difficult situation, weighing the value of going to school, getting a job, and having to pay off student loans.

This in turn can have a negative effect on the couple's thinking about having children. If they delay the engagement and the wife earns a degree and ends up with student loans, they may be tempted to put off having children by various forms of birth control so that she can use her degree or so that they can pay down her student loans. This may mean that they don't start having children until their thirties, or that they choose to keep their children in day care so that Mom can pursue her career.

All these are good reasons not to delay an engagement. I realize that some don't start dating until later in life. But for those who are seriously dating at a younger age, don't push this off.

DeYoung has some strong words especially for young men who put off dating and engagement:

When there is an overabundance of Christian singles who want to be married, this is a problem. And it's a problem I put squarely at the feet of young men whose immaturity, passivity, and indecision are pushing their hormones to the limits of self-control, delaying the growing-up process, and forcing countless numbers of young women to spend lots of time and money pursuing a career (which is not necessarily wrong) when they would rather be getting married and having children. Men, if you want to be married, find a godly gal, treat her right, talk to her parents, pop the question, [and] tie the knot.[5]

LEAVING

One important passage that must be considered by engaged couples as they prepare for marriage is found in Genesis 2:24: "Therefore shall a man leave his father and his mother, and shall cleave unto his wife: and they shall be one flesh." The first thing this word of God requires is that if we are going to get married, we must be ready to leave father and mother.

Understand what this does not mean. It certainly does not mean that we are utterly to abandon or forsake our parents. We must still have an attitude of respect for our parents. Children also have the responsibility of caring for their parents when they get old and struggle with health problems. Neither does leaving father and mother simply mean that children move out of the house when they get married or that they move a long distance away from their parents. There are

---

5   DeYoung, Just Do Something, 108.

some people who have moved to the other side of the world and still have not left their parents. There are others who live right next door to their parents and have truly left father and mother. It is not a matter of distance.

So what does it mean to leave father and mother? Leaving father and mother involves a radical change in your relationship to your parents. Before, you were under their authority and dependent upon them, but now that changes. You are no longer under their authority as you were before. You are not dependent upon them like before. You are not dependent upon their affection, assistance, and advice anymore. You establish an adult relationship with them. Your relationship becomes more one of friends than one of authority.

This says something again about the closeness and intimacy of marriage. The parent-child relationship is extremely close. It's so close because we are the flesh and blood of our parents. They gave birth to us and raised us. But the parent-child relationship is not the most important relationship. The closest earthly relationship is not the bond of flesh and blood, but the bond of marriage, the union of two people who have no blood connection to each other. This is amazing! If that's true, then just as we are horrified by a parent abandoning a child, we ought to be just as horrified by a spouse abandoning another spouse.

Some very serious dangers have to be avoided here. It can be a temptation, often early on in marriage, for married couples still to cleave to father and mother. This can be done in any number of ways. Married persons might be dependent upon their parents for advice and help in an unhealthy way. A wife might talk to her mother about all sorts of intimate things without ever talking to her husband about them. A husband might go and talk to his dad about an issue he is having without ever talking to his wife.

Another danger is that married persons live for their parents' approval and affection. They want to do everything so that their parents will approve. She might want to have the perfectly designed home and the model children so that her parents approve. He wants to make a lot of money or have a successful career or follow in the family business to make his dad happy.

This unhealthy cleaving might show itself in trying to change your spouse to be what your parents want. The husband might try to change his wife so that she is just like his mother, and a wife might try to change her husband so that he is just like her dad. He might tell his wife that she'd better cook the way his mother does because she is the best cook. She might tell her husband that he has to be handier around the house because her dad is.

This cleaving might show itself in the way we do things. A husband might do certain things because that's the way his dad did it and it must be the right way. A wife might do certain things because that's the way her mom did it and it must be the right way. When they get into an argument, the husband blows up in anger because that's the way his parents handled their issues. But the wife bottles up and runs away because that's the way things were dealt with by her parents. He has no problem spending money because that's the way it went in his house, and she is extremely tight because that's the way her parents were.

When children don't leave father and mother (and when the parents don't let them leave!), this is disastrous for a marriage. The married couple might think that they are showing respect to their parents. Or they might not think about what they are doing at all. But the result of their cleaving to dad and mom is that they are hurting their marriage. The failure to leave father and mother has even been the cause of the destruction of marriages!

When you get engaged, you must be ready to leave father and mother! And when you get married, you must actually leave them, with all that that entails.

CLEAVING

Genesis 2:24 says not only that couples must be ready to leave father and mother when they get married, but they must also be ready to "cleave" to their spouse and "be one flesh."

To "cleave" means to cling to something, to hold it very close to you, and to protect it with your life. The word used here literally means to be glued to someone. A man is glued to his wife so that the two stick to each other. This is real love in marriage. Love is not fundamentally a feeling, because feelings come and go. But love is a commitment to cleave to each other.

This means that husbands and wives must strive to be one in marriage. On the one hand, this oneness is a reality in marriage, but on the other hand, this oneness is something that must be worked at. Such oneness does not come easily, because there are many things that tear at this unity. This means that there is a constant calling for married couples to work together toward greater oneness.

So how will you have to work at your marriage? This need to work at their marriage is often the well-intended advice that young couples are given on their wedding day, but what does this mean practically? Here are five practical suggestions for you to consider as you look forward to marriage.

1. Recognize and root out all the things that get in the way.

Obviously what tears at the oneness of marriage is sin. Our pride, selfishness, self-righteousness, breaking of trust, anger, frustration, and all the rest tear us apart rather than bring us together. This means that there must be regular confession of sin to one another and regular forgiveness that is extended to one another. We must be mindful of our sins and root them out of our marriages.

Another threat to marriage is busyness. We live in an age where there are many technological advances that make life easier, and yet we are busier than we have ever been before. Both husband and wife have their careers, there is work being done on the house, the kids are in sports and in music lessons, and there are recreations we want to enjoy. Add to that all the spiritual activities: school board meetings, Mother's Circle meetings, council meetings, Bible study, catechism, church functions. We are so busy that our marriages are placed on the sideline and given no attention. We are two ships passing in the night.

Another marriage killer is having separate lives: separate families, separate friends, separate interests, separate finances. This is not living together; this is living independently.

Recognize these unity killers, and root them out.

2. View your marriage as a priority.

We must see this as our most important relationship aside from our relationship to Christ. Too often couples are simply coexisting in their marriage. They simply live under the same roof. More time and energy is placed into their job than into each other. More time and energy is placed into friendships with others than into their relationship within the bond of marriage.

One of the great dangers is that we prioritize our relationship with our children over our spouse. We spend all our time thinking about the children, talking with them, and doing things with them. What often happens is that when the children move out, husband and wife have no relationship with each other. They hardly know the person to whom they are married.

This demands a massive shift in our thinking. We must prioritize our marriage. We must view our spouse as our best friend. Our primary concern is for our marriage: this is what receives the most attention, this is where we find the most joy, this is where we share ourselves, this is where we look for guidance and advice and encouragement and comfort. We are concerned about being a good son or daughter to our parents, but this comes second to our concern about being a good spouse. We are concerned about being a good parent to our children if God has given them, but this too comes second to our concern about being a good spouse.

3. Spend time together.

Failure to heed this suggestion may especially be a danger for husbands. After all, God commands husbands to "dwell with [their wives] according to knowledge" (1 Pet. 3:7). Husbands work long hours at their job. They are gone at night for conferences or business trips. Maybe they also serve on school board or on church council. Rather than coming home after work and their other responsibilities, they might be tempted to go out with their buddies to have a beer and shoot the breeze. Husbands must guard against these things, balance their home and work life carefully, and be devoted to spending time with their wives.

This time together must be *meaningful*. Sitting together for an hour every night watching Netflix before crashing in bed hardly qualifies as quality time.

There must be time spent together *daily*. Some days this is more difficult than others, but there has to be a conscious effort to spend time with one another.

There must be time spent *alone*, without the children. It is healthy if every month you get a sitter and go out for dinner or go for a walk together. Once in a while it is good to drop the kids off at your parents so that you can go overnight somewhere. Call it a "date," call it a break, but whatever you call it, make time for it.

4. Converse constantly.

Husbands and wives ought to talk to one another about everything. Nothing is off-limits. You ought to know everything about your spouse and about what is going on in his or her life.

Every day you should have a daily briefing on what has happened in the day. But when you talk, the conversation ought to be more than just talk about your job or about the latest issue with your kids. At some point you should also talk about other things: about your marriage, about your common interests, about your goals and plans, about your sorrows and discouragements.

This means that you turn to one another for advice and emotional support. You don't immediately turn to parents or friends for this, but you first work things out with your spouse and support one another emotionally.

5. Grow together spiritually.

The foundation of our marriages is our spiritual oneness. If we are not growing together spiritually, then nothing else we do is really going to draw us closer together. God is the one who unites us together, and if we are not growing in our walk with him, we cannot expect to grow together.

This means we take time daily to pray together. We don't just pray for each other, we don't just pray with our children, but we need time together on our knees to pray for our marriages.

This also means that we are seeking to grow spiritually. We go to church and discuss the sermons together. We have family devotions and talk about God's word. We read spiritual things and discuss what we have read. We encourage one another in spiritual things.

To cleave to each other in marriage takes a lot of work. We cannot coast along, but we must constantly be working at our marriages. We must constantly be applying the glue that binds us to our spouse. Every marriage is moving either toward isolation or toward oneness. We must be intentional and proactive in cleaving to one another.

DISCUSSION QUESTIONS

1. What things ought to characterize a relationship in each of the stages listed?

2. What things do we need to remember about breakups?

3. What fears do you have about getting married? Why is it important to leave father and mother when you get married?

4. In what practical ways do we cleave to our spouse in marriage?

5. What things have you learned about dating differently from reading this book?

CONCLUSION

As you're probably aware, the book of Proverbs was written with young people specifically in view. Solomon, under the inspiration of the Holy Spirit, gives instruction to his son concerning every area of earthly life, including instruction regarding sex and marriage.

As you're probably also aware, Proverbs has as its overarching theme the subject of wisdom. For example, Proverbs 4:7 says, "Wisdom is the principal thing; therefore get wisdom: and with all thy getting get understanding." To help my little children understand what wisdom is, I often tell them it is knowing what's right and doing what's right. Wisdom is seeking to glorify God in all of one's life.

The will of God for young people (and adults) is that they be characterized by wisdom. How vital that young people be wise! That they seek to glorify God in all their life!

My desire with this brief book is that God would use it to make you wiser, specifically in your dating. My hope is that you would date more carefully, more deliberately, and more chastely. I would be thrilled to know that even one young person, having read this book, sought more consciously to glorify God as he or she pursued marriage.

For that purpose I've attempted to point you throughout the book to the basic principles of God's word. Only the infallibly inspired scriptures "are able to make thee wise unto salvation" (2 Tim. 3:15). Let that word be the lamp unto your feet and the light unto your path in dating, singleness, and marriage.

Also with the purpose in view of wise Christian daters, I've attempted to make this book very practical and down-to-earth. As much as possible I've tried to help you see how the principles of God's word work themselves out in the day-to-day of dating. I've purposely set the bar high and been idealistic with certain things, so that you would aim high in your dating. This means, as with everything you read, be discerning. In expressing my opinion on certain matters, I don't in any way want to promote a kind of legalism where you think you must follow all my man-made judgments. By all means, reject what I suggest if it is not fitting or realistic. But, by all means, follow the principles of God's word and aim in your dating for the glory of God.

My prayer is that, having dated wisely for God's glory, you would also live in marriage wisely for God's glory. At the beginning of the book, we learned that dating differently means dating with marriage in view and doing so for God's glory. In striving by the grace of God to date this way, you will find that he also gives the grace to live in marriage as he would have you to live. Though marriage can be challenging and requires much hard work, when you are striving by God's grace to live as he calls us to, it is a source of tremendous joy. The man and his wife are truly "happy" and "blessed" (Ps. 128). But more than our own happiness, our marriages will serve their ultimate purpose: the glory of our God in the demonstration of the unity of the Bridegroom and his Bride.

NOTES

NOTES

NOTES

Looking for a good book on marriage?
Consider one of these titles!

Better to Marry: Sex and Marriage in 1 Corinthians 6 & 7
by David J. Engelsma

Straightforward, practical instruction for single and married believers alike, taken directly from the classic Bible passages on sex and marriage.

> "...whether single or married, [Christians] would do well to read and apply the down-to-earth practical instruction that one finds in this book."
>
> –Rev. Audred Spriensma
> in *The Standard Bearer*

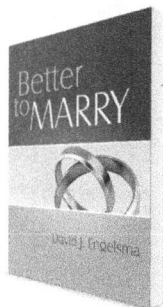

128 pages
paperback
ISBN 978-1-936054-38-1

◆

Marriage, The Mystery of Christ and the Church
by David J. Engelsma

A Reformed pastor's instruction and exhortation to young married couples that they glorify God in their marriages and enjoy the bliss of this blessed communion of life.

> "This is one of those books that you wish could be put into the hands of every married couple and those contemplating marriage..."
>
> –*The Gospel Witness*

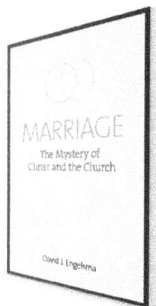

256 pages
paperback
ISBN 978-1-936054-51-0

Visit rfpa.org to place your order!
Also available in ebook format.

www.ingramcontent.com/pod-product-compliance
Lightning Source LLC
Chambersburg PA
CBHW071345090426
42738CB00012B/3016